EXISTENTIALIST THINKERS AND THOUGHT

Existentialist
THINKERS
and
THOUGHT

by FREDERICK PATKA

THE CITADEL PRESS
Secaucus, New Jersey

Fourth paperbound printing, 1972
Published by Citadel Press, Inc.
A subsidiary of Lyle Stuart, Inc.
120 Enterprise Ave., Secaucus, N.J. 07094
Copyright © 1962 by Philosophical Library, Inc.
Manufactured in the United States of America
ISBN 0-8065-0157-X

CONTENTS

Eugene J. Fitzgerald, *LaSalle College*

Thomas Gallagher, *Chestnut Hill College*
Heinz Moenkemeyer, *University of Pennsylvania*
Donald A. Gallagher, *Villanova University*
Joseph Mihalich, *LaSalle College*

PREFACE

Ever since the *WHY* divinely-spoken in Paradise under-scored the first of the problems facing mankind in the uni-verse of human experience, man has been seeking satisfactory solutions to the multiplicity of whys presented throughout successive ages. Kaleidoscopically shifting patterns of human experience have compelled each of these ages to make adjust-ments incorporating new factors; and man's thought—as a result of this—grew, developed, evolved.

Twentieth Century man stands at the apex of centuries which have coped with the great problems of mankind. He has the benefit of wisdom offered by the great minds of the past; he has seemingly new and challenging problems loom-ing on distant horizons. He has applied his own reasoning, his own convictions, his own explanations to formulate his own body of explanatory thought—his philosophy. Although this age, as every age preceding it, is characterized by mul-tiple philosophical theories, we do find a dominant trend in the main stream of current philosophy. This philosophy we term Existentialism.

The *Logos*—Philosophy Club of Holy Family College, under the leadership of Dr. Frederick Patka, Chairman of the Philosophy Department and club moderator, undertook in 1960 to bring philosophy "down to earth" for the benefit of college students and all others interested. It chose Existen-tialism as the central theme for its lectures and discussions to provide deeper insight into contemporary philosophy of life without, however, losing sight of its historical indebtedness to the *philosophia perennis* as a guiding post of critical evaluations.

1

Dealing with the historical and cultural background of existential thinking, Dr. Patka himself presented the first five lectures as a foundation for understanding the subsequent five about individual existentialists. These were delivered by guest speakers, each particularly qualified, all valuable contributors.

This volume, *Logos Lecture Series I*, incorporates the ten lectures which constituted the first annual program, the *Institute on the Philosophy of Life or Existence*. Having attracted an interested clientele in their original format, that of prepared talks, these lectures will assuredly prove a valuable contribution toward broadening cultural horizons at this new format, that of published articles.

Holy Family College is deeply aware of the need for enrichment of thought, of life itself, through philosophy as a concomitant — a fundamental concomitant — of totality in education.

On behalf of Holy Family College, therefore, I acknowledge and highly commend the genuine and valuable contribution made to the *Logos* program specifically and to the furthering of interest in philosophy generally by the outstanding contributors:

Frederick Patka, Ph.D., Chairman of the Philosophy Dept., Holy Family College

Eugene J. Fitzgerald, B.A., Cand. Ph.D., Assistant Professor of Philosophy, La Salle College

Donald A. Gallagher, Ph.D., Vice-Chairman of Department of Philosophy, Graduate School of Villanova University

Thomas Gallagher, Ph.D., Assistant Professor of Philosophy, Chestnut Hill College

Joseph M. Mihalich, M.A., Cand. Ph.D., Assistant Professor of Philosophy, La Salle College

Heinz Moenkmeyer, Ph.D., Assistant Professor of German, University of Pennsylvania

An expression of appreciation is due Dr. Austin App, Associate Professor of English at La Salle College who contributed services as an introductory speaker.

Appreciative recognition is extended also to the young ladies, *Logos* club members and other students of Holy Family College, who have contributed to the success of the program and subsequently to this publication through service in various capacities: as usherettes, hostesses, mailing clerks, typists, transcribers, and editors.

To all contributors I extend my deep and sincere thanks. Their efforts have enabled Holy Family College to offer its students a much deeper experience in philosophical insights as a complement to academic course offerings. To students and guests alike, they have extended the opportunity for cultural self-appropriation as a means to a richer, more meaningful life.

Sister M. Aloysius, C.S.F.N.
President

INTRODUCTION

Philosophy is the road to wisdom.

Wisdom is appropriated by the process of ascending insights into the problems of man's existence, his world, and his Creator. Insights may occur on different levels of integration, such as common sense, science, and philosophy. Each level stands for a specific profile of existence and cultural horizon. Undoubtedly, it is philosophic insight which provides man with the critical, reflective, and ultimate experience of cultural self-appropriation as the practical goal of philosophizing.

Shall we justify and put up reasons—perhaps excuses—and apologies for presenting philosophy as man's highest form of cultural achievement? From the standpoint of a historical consciousness, no apologies are needed. Philosophy—under different names or labels—has always been with us, even though it may not have been called or recognized as such. We call it *"philosophia perennis"*—perennial philosophy as man's continuous quest for rational self-appropriation. In this sense, universal philosophy, including existentialism or the philosophy of life, is not ancient, medieval, modern or contemporary; it is not fashionable today and outmoded tomorrow. Being perennial, philosophy is always the same due to the basic identity of human nature, even though the problems analyzed and the solutions proposed may cover a wide range of antagonistic doctrines. In this historical perspective we say that perennial philosophy does not need justification, and it does not have to apologize for being with us. It has always been with us, and it will always be with us, as long as there will be man whose definition is rational, *homo sapiens.*

However, from the point of view of the present-day socio-economic situation, philosophy should perhaps ask for permission to appear in public. In the eyes of many contemporaries, philosophy seems to be old-fashioned, academic, too abstract, and removed from the every-day rush of modern living. Because of the pragmatic, economic, and utilitarian atmosphere created by modern technology and science, philosophy is forced to lead a pseudo-existence. It may exist in the libraries, in books which are seldom opened and read. It has a lonely existence on the shelves where only dust keeps it company. Philosophy may also exist in required courses in certain college curricula. However, "required" philosophy courses do not represent philosophy because they are not integrated into one's existential concerns. Philosophy is not experienced as a challenge to one changing his life. It is just theory, a set of principles thrown at the students. Perhaps it is forced down one's throat. But this method will bring about some sort of a psychic indigestion. In any case, this is not the philosophy we have in mind and wish to present to our readers.

You will not find philosophy on the market place. You will not find it in the mentality of the extrovert, self-estranged forms of modern self-deception. You will not find philosophy in the crowd and in the places frequented by the crowd. For philosophy has always been aristocratic, an intellectual nobility—the nobility of certain men being possessors or at least lovers of wisdom. Now, it is this intellectual nobility, practiced on an individual basis, which disappears in the crowd in order to give place to emotional forms of thinking and pragmatic valuing.

It is not easy to find philosophy today in the modern office of the physician, psychologist, psychiatrist, social worker or progressive educationist. All these highly specialized professionals claim to be just scientists and not philosophers. Philosophy is being considered by them as an archeological sample of medieval obscurantism. Philosophy not being modern must be rejected.

You will not find philosophy in the office of the economic man either, nor in the concern of the business manager nor on the shelves of supermarkets and drug stores. Similarly, you will not find philosophy on the television screen, for it cannot be "rigged." The other media of mass communication can do without philosophy; it is not a popular consumer's good wanted by the millions and advertised for millions with a money back guarantee. Besides, they argue, philosophy is not for the average mediocrity; it can not be measured by the lowest standards of common wants. At the most, philosophy can be the intellectual hobby of a few snobs, that is, socially maladjusted individuals. . . .

Where is philosophy to be found then? One may find philosophy as a personal experience, if that individual can measure up to the ideals of being a self-conscious, rational existent. In that case, philosophy may appear as the invisible spirit of life-integration, informing every aspect of one's existence.

Human existence can be lived on different levels of personal or social integration. Many persons, too many, vegetate. Many others add to this mere vegetation the pleasures of sensate experiences. Some truly enlightened persons may reach the horizon of a critical evaluation of their being in all its aspects and implications.

Life on the level of simple vegetation—if practiced by human beings—leads necessarily to a primitive, prelogical, and earth-bound concern of the animal who divorced himself from his innate nobility as a rational being. The vegetative outlook on life is dominated by the pleasure principle of the practical hedonist. The same should be our value judgment regarding life lived on the sensate level.

Man may live his life also on the rational, analytic, critical, and scientific levels. This move already demonstrates man's emancipation from his original condition of pure animality. Rational emancipation could nevertheless present a new danger of personal self-estrangement, mainly if its concern will be restricted to the theoretical formulations of individual experiences. As soon as we formulate something in theory, abstraction is used. Abstraction is—by its very nature —a removal from life's original and total reality. One learns, for instance, that man is a rational animal. This statement holds true in theory but in theory only. This abstract definition of man in general does not embrace the individual existent as a singular, unique, and original instance of existence. Is one's existence a theoretical definition or is it rather a particular situation or condition to be approached rather intuitively than abstractly?

Above the rational, abstract, and universal theory of life there is a further synthesis. We may call this the third level of integration consisting in the reflective questioning of the validity of the previous forms of integrations. This reflective questioning is aimed at the ultimate validation of individual and social existence. This new frame of mind reaches beyond the wisdom of common sense and scientific rationalism. It does not deny their validity but it subjects them to the scrutiny of reflective reconsiderations of generally accepted principles. We believe that it is at this point that the philosophic integration of life begins. It is the transition from immediate insights provided by common sense and science to the new horizon of ultimate reasons, the reality of the unconditioned experience, which gives validity to the more inferior forms of knowledge. It is a new judgment of value about the value of the value judgments—beliefs, proverbial wisdom, common sense, and scientific theory.

The reflective reconsideration of human insights may not result in an integral synthesis of life. This is one lesson we may learn from the history of human ideas and so called "systems and schools" of philosophy. For the purpose of

8

illustration we may divide philosophers into two categories, each of them representing either *"Logos"*—the Idea—or *"Bios"*—life and existence. Almost at any historical period one may find "rational intellectualists" defending the priority and the primacy of *"Logos,"* creating systems of philosophy such as idealism or rationalism. On the other hand, there have been others who demanded more importance for and attention to the fate of the individual human existent with all his existential concerns demanding some solution. The latter have been known as philosophers of life or—in modern terminology—existentialists. The present collection of lectures will introduce the reader into the world of insights achieved by contemporary philosophers who stand for the priority of Life over and against the annihilating power of transcendental panlogism of the idealists.

Our method of presentation will concern itself first with the fundamental themes of modern existentialism in order to create a foundation for the understanding of individual existentialists, of whom we shall present five outstanding representatives: Kierkegaard, Heidegger, Jaspers, Sartre, and G. Marcel. Whenever possible, we shall draw comparisons between their mode of thinking and that of moderate realism which—we believe—represents the fortunate synthesis of both *"Logos"* and *"Bios."*

PART ONE

FIVE EXISTENTIALIST THEMES

By Frederick Patka
Holy Family College

THE PROBLEM OF KNOWLEDGE

THE GAP BETWEEN ABSTRACT REASONING AND LIFE

The beginner in the study of the history of human ideas will sooner or later experience a state of frustration, brought about by the great variety of philosophic doctrines, systems, and schools which seem to contradict one another's teachings. However, it takes more than a superficial reading of texts in the history of philosophy in order to discover, among the apparent disharmony of principles, *the law of organic continuity of ideas* which will lead to the discovery of an intelligent dialogue among philosophers throughout the centuries. Should this discovery be the lot of the student of philosophic systems, he will be able to see harmony, unity, and synthesis without the discomforting feeling of overall confusion.

The first requirement needed for the discovery of a meaningful evolution of human ideals and ideas is the adoption of the correct mental attitude, developed by the ability to see philosophy through the dimension of time and space as a dialectical procession in which every new idea, principle, and system answers to the position presented by the foregoing theme or moment. Answers, of course, are many. Some of them may represent definite commitments such as "yes" or "no"; others may represent just the state of wise suspense for the sake of safe immunity when saying, for instance, "maybe" or "I don't know."

A "yes" stands for affirmation, agreement, and it provides room for the positive development of the basic idea or doctrine thus accepted either by its intrinsic evidence or the worship of authority. "No," as a negative answer, represents denial, rejection, disagreement, and it imposes the further task of giving reasons for one's opposition to a given principle. Here again the rejection may be inspired either by logical insights into the insufficiency of the doctrine presented or personal bias, emotionally supported. Finally, the absence of final commitment in the mind of skeptics reveals the presence of an either honest or dishonest doubt. Whatever the reactions may be, they create the foundations of dialectics whose antagonistic structure includes a position "thesis," an opposition "antithesis," and hopes for some solution—"synthesis" as the coexistence of opposites in a temporary balance. This is what is meant by the law of organic continuity of ideas in a historical perspective and it is this methodical approach we shall use in introducing existentialism on the stage of philosophic dialectics.

Existentialism or philosophy of life stands as a vigorous "no"; it is a vehement protest, a radical reaction against two previous philosophic systems. On the one hand existentialism wages war against all kinds of scientific positivism, materialism, and technological pragmatism, accusing them of the crime of having killed the true spirit of human culture by reducing man's highest values and ideals to mere sublimation of animal instincts. Existentialism wants to discredit the basic assumptions and applied conclusions of philosophic idealism as well, especially the transcendental panlogism of Hegel, as the ultimate expression and extreme case of rationalism, intellectualism, and monistic pantheism. Both systems fought against by existentialism have one common assumption. It is the absolute primacy and superiority of man's

14

reason and intellect over the rest of man's psychic dispositions, such as imagination, feelings, and intuition. Consequently, it is at this point that existentialism starts its attack on either empiricism or metaphysical idealism. It is this strategic position of the existentialists which lends their warfare a definite anti-intellectual, anti-rational character. It is the protest of *"Bios"*—Life, against *"Logos"*—reason. The contention is that *"Logos"* can not account for the complexity of *"Bios,"* being, therefore, an inadequate instrument for the philosopher who wants to present a realistic account of life and existence. Hence, the importance of the doctrine on the nature of human knowledge as the prolegomenon to the presentation of man's true existential condition. Before going into the details of this fundamental assumption, its adequate treatment imposes the task of describing first the indictment of intellectualism by the philosophers of life.

The case the existentialists have against Hegel implies both his theoretical assumptions about the nature of human knowledge and its practical conclusions as well. On the theoretical level all idealists maintain the principle of immanence as their fundamental thesis. Following Kant's account of the make-up and the functioning of pure reason, all modern idealists teach man's failure to know reality in itself. Man knows only the internal object of knowledge whose being consists in being known. The immediate consequence is seen in the intraversion, subjectivization, and idealization of all reality, along with the negation of any transcendence. There is no objective reality independent of the knowing subject, and there is no way to break through the belt of subjectivity into a region of transcendent, metaphysical reality. In such way, the subject becomes the center and the creative source of all reality as such.

The principle of immanence brings about the worship of human reason as the creator of all that is or will be. The idolatry of human reason is completed by Hegel by identifying it with *Logos,* the Absolute Reason, the Absolute Idea

15

or the Absolute Spirit. However, Hegel's deification of Reason results actually in the devaluation of the human person. In his idealistic pantheism man as an individual human being appears now as the "trick of nature," only an insignificant moment, a temporary period of transition, a contingent element in the eternal process of evolution of the Absolute Reason, *Logos*.

The existentialists identify their philosophic mission as the quest for the rehabilitation of man's value as an individual existent whose existential situation—if adequately analyzed—appears to be the direct denial of all the logical and metaphysical categories belonging to the historical unfolding of Hegel's Absolute Reason. The individual existent is a concrete, singular, unique, original, free, and responsible person, As such he is opposed to the abstract, universal, identical, necessary and eternal reality of *Logos* in its eternal process of dialectical manifestations. In one word, man as a contingent, finite, and transient being represents *"Bios"*— Life in all its concreteness and singularity, whereas *Logos* stands for the abstract life of the intellect, extrapolated, hypostatized as the Absolute Spirit of logical necessities.

Every reaction, even in the history of philosophy, possesses some of the impatient spirit of radical reformers and revolutionaries. Therefore, it is more than likely to fall into the other extreme position, thus committing the same mistake they are trying to remedy. Unfortunately, this has been true of the existentialists also. While reacting against the excesses of transcendental idealism, they have gone too far by discrediting man's intellect and presenting it as altogether unfit for the task of true philosophizing. What they have to present as a substitute for the intellect looks not much better either. We shall first describe the anti-intellectual attitude of the existentialists; then, shall proceed with the analysis of the new kind of knowledge, intuition, as proposed by the philosophers of life, especially Bergson.

According to the existentialists, man's intellect is meant

16

by nature to be nothing more than a practical tool or instrument for the adaptation of the original, everchanging reality to the needs of practical action of the *"homo faber,"* the laborer. This is accomplished first, by freezing the fluid reality in the forms of static immobility required for successful manipulation of nature. Objects are created by substituting man's logical categories for the dynamic *"élan vital"* of original reality. The intellect will clear the ground selectively by imposing arbitrarily upon the amorphous reality of changing phenomena its own logical forms, such as: identity, relation, cause, effect, regularity, immobility, quantity, consistency, universality, validity, and so forth. It is pragmatic action which demands this strictly logical organization of reality in logical forms which is the condition for man's success in trying to dominate and manipulate matter, time, and energy. In such manner, the universal prevails over the individual phenomena; the validity of scientific laws and principles make projected action not only possible but successful as well. The intellect appears, therefore, as the organizing power subjected to the demands of pragmatic needs and concerns.

There are several conclusions the existentialists draw from their assumption about the nature of human intellect "according to the intention of Nature":

The process of intellectual knowledge is not conformity to an intelligible order of beings; it is not the correspondence between the subject and the object of knowledge either. Man's intellect does not discover, reveal, or unravel objective truth; its natural tendency consists in "intelligent" foresight instead of insight. It projects itself into the possibilities of future action for whose success it draws the practical blueprint. By the same token, the intellect's creativity is confined to the concerns of pragmatic projection into the future demands imposed on it by the imperative of efficient doing and making. Given this predominance of useful activism over the detached analysis of pure reason in the

17

make-up of the *"homo faber,"* it appears untrue to claim any privileged situation for man's reaching power. In the saying of Bergson: *"l'action prime la connaissance,"* the action dominates knowledge.

Consequently, our universal concepts do not represent "essences" of known objects; they answer only to a merely practical question about what use one can make of known things. Interest and necessity appear to be the *a priori* conditions for the possibility of useful knowledge. A similar value judgment applies also to the intrinsic nature of scientific method, its systematic research and discoveries. For the existentialists science is fundamentally positive, empirical, applied, and above all, a useful tool in the hands of men engaged in the conquest of physical reality. Scientific hypothesis, its fundamental principles and established laws stand as reliable guiding systems in man's endeavor to create civilization. The disengaged world of the scientist, the love of knowledge for the knowledge's sake, a passionate pursuit of more knowledge and insight are incompatible with the utilitarian and materialistic concern of practical information provided by the intellect.

Thus, the value of intellectual knowledge becomes necessarily subjective and relative, insofar as it is specified by the organic needs of active subjects. Being relative, it also implies its imperfect, deficient character for dwelling only in the superficial, common aspects of things to be manipulated. Moreover, it is just "symbolic" in the sense of adapting and thereby distorting the immaculate originality of true reality understood as a constant flux, or change *(écoulement)*, and creative evolution.

The final verdict of the existentialists concerning intellectual knowledge has to be its irreversible indictment and rejection. A kind of knowledge—we are told—dominated completely by the imperative of usefulness is *a priori* unfit for true philosophizing aimed at the reconstruction of realistic metaphysics. The intellect's inadequacy is further emphasized by calling attention to the plurality of contradictory schools and systems of philosophy, agitating pseudo-problems without realizing that no one can reconstruct reality in itself from mere symbols. Human concepts, being only useful symbols subservient to economic, technical, and industrial purposes, will never lead to what they symbolize.

The existentialists' painstaking polemic is aimed simultaneously against the excesses of scientific positivism and transcendental idealism. It is an aggressive attitude toward nineteenth century materialism and logistic pantheism. By discrediting intellect and reason, the existentialists hope to deliver a deadly blow to their prestige achieved in the minds of both scientific rationalists and transcendental idealists. This emotionally inspired hostility applies to all and any kind of "doctrine," "theory," "system," "school," "*Weltanschauung*," presented as the "final" achievement and synthesis of human knowledge as such.

Having debased intellectual knowledge to the level of mere subjective and relative symbolism, the existentialists gladly announce the discovery of a new type of knowledge which is free of all deficiencies ascribed to man's practical thinking. This new type of knowledge is called intuition.

The existence of intuition is not demonstrated; it is simply postulated and vigorously defended. Being radically different from intellectual knowledge, there is no way to define it in universal terms and concepts. The existentialists also acknowledge the common man's difficulty in rising above the level of intellectual practicality, a move needed for the experience of intuitive knowledge of genuine reality. Those who experience it may describe it in different ways.

Bergson introduces intuition as a form of "intellectual sympathy," a spiritual auscultation of living reality, first within the depths of the individual person, then in the rhythm of nature itself. Considering first the psychological process through which intuition as an act of knowledge takes its form, we should point out its simplicity. It is a single, total, and dynamic attitude directed at the totality of being in the constant process of becoming and evolving. The proper object of intuition is not restricted to one or another "aspect" of the real; it encompasses, embraces the simplicity of the real without freezing it in separate pieces of particular information.

From the standpoint of the knower's intention, intuition appears as a detached, disinterested, almost unselfish listening to the manifestation of being in its originality. The success of being able to listen and to hear something presupposes a certain superior form of inner sensitivity and suggestibility which prepares the subject for "receiving" the revelation of being as it is in itself without any degree of distortion by the subject's psychic dispositions. The correct attitude also requires a total dedication of man's whole being; the act of intuition is not the activity of any one psychic disposition taken apart from the subject's total structural make-up. On the contrary, it is the global cooperation of cognitive, affective, emotional, and volitive tendencies aimed at the mutual copenetration of the knower with the known. Thus, the duality of subject-object relationship is eliminated: the subject lives the life of the object from within and gathers his integral insights at the source of being, all being.

The outcome of this silent introspection and subject-object identification is described as the emergence of manifestation of a new reality, apprehended in its totality as a living becoming which progressively engulfs ever new profiles and horizons of existence. As to its value, intuition is commended as absolute and perfect. There is only one deficiency and that concerns the possibilities of communication of one's experiences in the depths of being. Since universal concepts and ideas are mere instrumentalities subordinated to the needs of practical life adjustment, the existentialists must make use of the metaphor, analogy, and symbolic imagery. Some of them prefer the use of literary art and style believing that certain aspects of existence are better shown and illustrated by dramatic representation than in the form of traditional use of language. Their literary style is rich in the use of adjectives and words describing attitudes, experiences; while nouns score much lower in their vocabulary. The distrust of logical reasoning introduces the claim for a pre-logical, pre-judicial, pre-conceptual form of intuitive awareness which discloses the full, concrete, living, purely qualitative, and absolute pulsation of evolving reality. The end result of sustained intuition should be the institution of a new metaphysics to be identified as the "integral experience of Being."

In order to illustrate further both the anti-intellectual tendency of existentialism and its exclusive concern with intuition as revelatory of being, it may be helpful to oppose the conflicting pairs of traditional philosophy and the new one, respectively.

The particular, singular, unique, exclusive, individual, concrete, and personal experiences of the existentialists are opposed to the universal, abstract, theoretical, logical, common, general, impersonal, uniform, identical and systematic concepts, laws, and principles of the intellectualists.

Existentialists have a definite preference for the new, original, a-typical, and emotionally charged complexity of situations in which the true existential condition of the free person is manifested at its best. Being aggressive thinkers, they choose rather the problematic, exceptional, marginal, at times even eccentric contents of human life leading up to the boundaries of the morbid and abnormal. Their emotional dispositions—concern, anxiety, dread, and loneliness—condition them to be prepared to expect and to experience the irrational, dangerous, and disrupting dimensions of existence. All these attitudes are negatively reinforced by a profound dislike of and contempt for the well organized, safe, secure, systematic, conservative, traditional, and philistine way of life led by the majority of just individuals as victims of habitual self-deceptions. In other words, the

21

existentialists claim to know more about the true meaning of existence than people used to know.

Before leaving this subject we should summarize our considerations by drawing a comparative parallel between the work accomplished by modern existentialists in the field of knowledge on the one hand, and Kant's achievements on the other.

Both Kant and the existentialists devaluate man's conceptual intellect. Kant teaches that it is the business of pure reason to organize and unify the data of sense experience by taking it into or under the a priori forms of understanding, called "categories." Moreover, Kant believes that the activity of pure reason makes objective rational science possible, though it never reaches into the things themselves. The existentialists also ascribe to intellect the task of logical organization. However, they maintain a purely pragmatic interpretation of this process, thus denying the objective value of scientific knowledge.

Kant denies intuition of the intellect; the existentialists describe it in superlatives. At a closer analysis, however, it appears that the existentialists attribute to intuition almost the same characteristics by which Kant used to describe the nature of "practical reason," man's judicial power. Kant believed it possible to reach the Absolute by means of the "practical reason," not in a logical demonstration but rather by a postulatory leap dictated by moral and religious convictions.

Kant maintained the duality of and mutual dependence between concepts and intuition, saying that concepts are empty without intuition, and that intuition is blind without concepts. It is rather strange to read the same idea repeated by Bergson who teaches that there are things which only the intellect is capable of looking for but which it is not able to find by itself. These things, continues Bergson, are found only by intuition which would never look for them by itself.

Herein lies the fundamental error of existentialism. While

desperately trying to overcome the extremes of transcendental idealism, it introduces the same basic duality and polarity between intellect and intuition, thus committing the same mistake it set out to correct. It is due to this violent separation and opposition that the most desired goal of existentialism, i.e., the institution of metaphysics, still remains unattained.

THE PROBLEM OF REALITY
BEING VERSUS LIFE AS CONCRETE DURATION

Every school of philosophy obtains its admission into the history of human thinking by virtue of a body or system of doctrines which identify it as a new and original variation on the same recurring theme of being or not being. In fact, the fundamental problems of philosophy are relatively few since the dimensions of being point only to three regions of reality: God, man, and the universe. Accordingly, a philosophy may be called "new" only in the sense that it has to say something different on the same basic questions of existence.

On the other hand, the new and original character of a philosophic doctrine is always conditioned by certain basic assumptions, positions, or principles, usually preconceived in the mind of the leading thinkers, the founders of the new wisdom. These fundamental principles refer to the ultimate nature of man, his world, and that of a superior Being who gives meaning and ultimate end to both. Furthermore, the first principles adopted by any given philosopher should be analyzed and interpreted in the light of an adequate psychosocial and historical constellation, regarded as the immediate factors responsible for their actuality and significance. Finally, these basic hypotheses will determine the proper object, both material and formal, of the philosophy to be constructed, as well as its method and practical consequences to be applied to the particular instances of being. Consequently, adequate understanding and subsequent evaluation of any philosophy should start as a critical analysis of its first principles.

The philosopher's outlook on reality is one of the first positions which direct the whole process of philosophizing. It it, therefore, of paramount importance that we shall dedicate sufficient attention to what the existentialists have to say on the "original" nature of reality. Since we have identified existentialism as the "protest of life against reason," it will be not only helpful but also necessary to outline first the concept of reality as presented by the philosophers of the traditional, intellectual, and realistic schools. Thus we shall know better against what the existentialists protest. At the same time we shall be in a better position to understand the doctrine they have to propose on the "authentic" nature of reality.

1. The philosophy conceived by Aristotelian realists considers "being" as coextensive with "reality." Being as reality in general includes different orders, according to different degrees in perfection, which account for the different modes of being, such as matter, spirit, substance, accidents, etc. All the different orders and modes of beings are cognized as irreducibly distinct, while making up the whole hierarchy of beings so well kept apart by the hierarchy of different sciences which study a different region of reality.

The philosophers of life on the contrary, restrict the concept of reality to the sphere of "life" and its synonymous terms, such as "duration," "pure mutability," "continuous change and becoming," etc. Whatever does not possess the qualities of a "living reality," such as "things" or "objects," should be excluded from the field of the new philosophy. Preference should be given only to those sciences which study "vital phenomena," for instance, biology, psychology, and the sciences of the Spirit (*Geisteswissenschaften*), created by *W. Dilthey* and followers. Positive or natural sciences study the static, dead, and mechanical world of objects constructed by the practical leaning of the abstract intellect. Consequently, the reality constructed by scientists falls short of the goal of the philosopher engaged in the discovery of a deeper dimension of existence.

2. In a more specific sense, being is the first both in the order of existence and that of knowledge: the intelligible order and that of being are commensurate (*ens et verum convertuntur*). Being, therefore, stands as that transcendental form of perfection through which everything is made actual and actually known. Reality is known in its immediate and ultimate nature only insofar as it is being. The different proprieties, structural laws, categories, and special characteristics of reality are and can be made accessible to man only through the actuality of being. Consequently, "life" or "living reality" appears to be only a special mode of being, and it is identified as such only with reference to being in general.

Since the existentialists made "life" coextensive with all original reality, it follows that they have to maintain and apply the same ontological and logical primacy, priority of what they call first reality. Only they do not ascribe to any of the transcendental attributes and logical categories of being while describing its genuine form of existence. Life should be described as pure tendency (*élan vital, Trieb*), conation, drive, aspiration, creative evolution, pure becoming, and change which constantly endures. As such, reality as life is necessarily "a-logical," rather than "pre-logical"; it is "ontic" without being "ontological." It is devoid of all and any intrinsic intelligibility, since it does not possess any degree of logical structure. The existentialists believe that the intelligible order of beings, as presented by traditional logical analysts, does not disclose reality in its inner living originality. It only deals with a secondary, derived and static logical structure of "things" (*le tout fait*), similar to the condition of the ice on the surface of ever flowing water. . . . True philosophical knowledge of reality can be attained only if the derived reality of static beings becomes dissolved on the pattern of the progressive flux of life which obtains, therefore, an absolute primacy and self-sufficiency. Becoming comes before being. Reality comes-to-be before it is anything. In scholastic terms this means that the being in potency precedes being in act both ontologically and logically.

3. Following the ontological primacy and priority of being, reality is given independently of a knowing subject. Whatever the subject discovers in the process of knowledge belongs to the inner structure of the intelligible object which appears to possess, at least potentially, all the contents which specify and determine the act of knowing. The subject only assimilates the object by conforming to the special nature of the object to be known. The object exists prior to the process of being known. Moreover, in the act of knowing subject and object become one: the subject is the object known. This identity, however, does not imply any creative power in the subject. Critical reflection on the act of assimilating the objectively given will separate the subjective elements from the objective contents of acquired insights. That which is known is never made identical with the psychic process whereby information is obtained. Thus the distinction between the object and the subject of knowledge is kept clear in spite of their identity in the very act of knowledge.

The subject-object relationship looks quite different in the doctrine of the anti-intellectual philosophers. Given the absolute primacy and universality of "life" as an uninterrupted process of pure becoming, reality is not "given" in the experience of the knower. Knowledge now appears to be an act of creative activity by which reality is brought into existence. Herein one can see the complete inversion of the traditional point of view: it is the subject's creativity which specifies the contents of knowledge and not vice-versa. Actually there is no given object at all. Truth or true knowledge is not the correspondence between the known and the knower; it is rather the "invention" of the creative existent in the process of incommunicable intuition. Since there is no object which exists independently of the knowing subject, the duality and the real distinction between subject and object is eliminated. The subject does not know reality; rather he creates it through the vital and dynamic act of intuition. Strictly speaking, intuition means more than "living the life of the object"; it is living the life of an object created by the act of intuition.

There are several important consequences which follow from the new interpretation of true, philosophic knowledge of "reality." First, the creative power of the knowing subject reminds us of the doctrine of transcendental idealism in which the being of the object equals its being perceived and known. Furthermore, by eliminating the reality of the objects to be known by a subject, there is no way for speaking of objectively true knowledge. Truth becomes equal to the creative imagination of the subject. An impersonal, disengaged, and detached attitude, guided by the criteria of what is given in one's experience, becomes no more than wishful thinking or a contradictory attitude. Finally, it is the same to say that the subject "creates" reality, as to maintain, at least implicitly, the subjectivists' or relativists' position.

4. The philosophy of being as such is rightly considered the first or fundamental philosophy in the sense that "ontology" becomes the meeting ground and the foundation for all philosophic and scientific disciplines. Objective reality, understood as the totality of what is given as manifestations of being on the scale of participation, is indeed the measure of both theoretical and practical concerns of the human mind. Truth is both ontological and logical. The latter is only the discovery of what has always been there whether known or not. Even the practical field of philosophy, ethics, still maintains a close contact with the world of objects insofar as its formal object, "goodness" is one of the transcendental

27

attributes of being *(ens et bonum convertuntur)*. Accordingly, man's free choice and preference is directly made specific by the objective order of particular goods and the good of order whose foundation is the reality of being as such.

In an analogous way the "philosophy of life" becomes the first and fundamental philosophy for the existentialists. The basic difference between traditional philosophy and existentialism lies in the objective and subjective character of their theoretical and practical doctrines respectively. Life is the incommunicable experience of an individual existent who appears now to be free from all objective instances of critical reflection and objective validation. Since it is the individual subject who creates "his" reality, it follows that the categories of "objective truth and goodness" appear to be meaningless. The validity of these categories become altogether personal, individual, incommunicable, and all the same originally "true." The emphasis put on the creative power of the subject can be seen further in the "psychologization" or "biologization" of all cultural values, bringing about a state of anarchy as far as the validity of their value judgments is concerned. After all, one individual's valuing is not better and not worse than that of any other individual. Even if they appear to be mutually exclusive, because contradictory, their validity is still maintained for being the genuine revelation of a new, profound, and original reality known by the individual's creative intuition.

This state of things may give some explanation for the disturbing variety of opposite "existential" approaches to the eternal problems of philosophy. One will easily find among existentialists some whose teachings may fit any extreme attitude regarding the meaning of human existence. Subjectivists, relativists, skeptics, "absurdists," faithful believers, and cynical hedonists appear to claim the same degree of validity for their revelatory experiences in the domain of living reality. Before discussing the amount of validity one should grant to their conflicting views, it would perhaps be better to question their sincerity and seriousness.

The considerations presented in the preceding analysis were meant as a comparative study of the differences between traditional Aristotelian realism on one hand and contemporary existentialism on the other. At this point, however, it seems necessary to go directly to the description of the new reality, revealed to the intuitive eye of the existentialist philosopher in the state of an introspective analysis of the immediate facts or experiences given in the depths of personal consciousness.

It was the French philosopher, *H. Bergson* who gave the most adequate account of this reality as manifested by the contents of intuitive insights, in his work, *"Essai sur les données immédiates de la conscience."* Below the superficial layer of conscious awareness of the world, of solidified objects, is an intimate region apprehended as the uninterrupted flux or succession of conscious states, which can be best described as "concrete duration" or "life" itself engaged in the process of dynamic unfolding. The essential characteristics of this intimate experience are described by *Bergson* in terms of a total, completely homogeneous, and continuous flow (*écoulement*) of experiences in which the totality of one's existence is identified as the copenetration of past, present, and projected future. There is no break in the chain of inner experiences, since any previous state announces the subsequent which, in its turn, still contains its predecessor. Diametrically opposed to any attempt at the atomization of the organic unity of one's inner life, *Bergson* further emphasizes this global oneness of personal interiority by adding more qualities which should reveal it more adequately. Thus we learn through him that this inwardness of life or existence represents an irreversible process in which something always new appears, suggesting the condition of sustained conation, a dynamic tendency (*l'élan vital*), never repeating itself, but constantly aimed at fuller and deeper apprehension of life.

There are no quantitative elements which would make room for fragmentation, divisions, classifications, statistical arrangements, and previsions or practical provisions. Life as spontaneous conation is radically opposed to all quantitative, numerical, physico-mechanical, and static methods of interpretation. In such a way *Bergson* hoped to discredit the validity of psychological atomism and mechanical determinism which prevailed in the second half of the nineteenth century.

Bergson was no less concerned with the excesses committed by *Hegel's* pantheistic panlogism which annihilated the meaning of the free and individual existence by subjecting it to the necessary dialectical evolution of an absolute Logos. Since transcendental idealism was born out of the deification of the rational, logical, and intellectual, *Bergson* had no hesitation to deny all logical or intelligible structure of reality. By way of sweeping generalization he demands that all reality should be described and interpreted "after the model of the reality of our own person," that is, as constant flux and change, a *purum fieri*, an irreversible process of conation. Thus he arrives at a daring conclusion in saying that "mobility is everything, or nothing."

Should someone point to the evidence of common sense experience in which the quantitative, identical, static, and uniform seems to exceed by far the qualitative and ever changing reality claimed by *Bergson*, he will answer such an objection by his view on the nature of human intellect, which, according to nature's intention, creates the logically structured world of objects. As we saw in the preceding chapter, this schematic organization of reality by the intellect serves the purpose of preparing the field for a successful manipulation of and control over reality by action.

The foregoing discussion may lead to the formulation of the really important question about the persons who seem to be the only qualified individuals for the attainment of "authentic" reality. In fact, let us ask the question: "Who are the privileged few who know the way to the region of reality in itself, free of all misleading distortions?"

The philosophers of life, while trying to give a satisfactory answer to this legitimate question, will first tell us, in negative terms, who are the persons that cannot be introduced into the depths of first reality. There are the man of common sense, the scientist of a positivistic and mechanical leaning, the Aristotelian intellectualist, and the Hegelian idealists. They have failed to communicate the ultimate nature of reality because they had taken something secondary and derived, that is, reality artificially produced by practical reason, as standing for the original. Their mistake occurred because of the wrong evaluation of the nature and role of man's reason and intellect. Instead of discovering the purely pragmatic bent of practical thinking aimed exclusively at practical achievements in the world of material things and objects, the philosophers of previous schools believed that it reveals the essences, the universal logical structure of a given reality, the world of objects out there. Led by this illusion, they constructed a pseudo-philosophy after the pattern of schematic and systematic science. They failed to discover the true intention of nature while providing man with an efficient tool for the conquest of nature.

Speaking now in positive terms, the existentialists do not hide their conviction of being only themselves the first true philosophers who have discovered "authentic" reality below the superficial surface of a static and pragmatic objectivism. They do not hesitate either in condemning altogether the value of previous philosophic achievements. They go further by demanding that all forms of traditional realism and intellectualism be rejected and abandoned as the required condition for the attainment of the new philosophy.

The new philosophy of life does not want to be a systematic and scientific account of the intelligible being which is objectively given in man's experiences. On the contrary, existentialism wants to be only a "mental attitude," a new "spirit of philosophy" motivated by the necessity of transcending the mechanical tendency of pragmatic intellect. It in the individual's persistent conation to develop a new point of view by trying to see reality in the perspective of a continuous, uninterrupted duration and succession. Its practical goal is not academic, scientific, theoretical or speculative. It is rather a personal concern with the more liberal evolution of concrete individuality. For this reason reality is restricted to the experiences of personal existence whose depths must be explored by a new methodical survey.

This survey is an experimental method without being scientific. It is experimental in the sense that it refers to *"une expérience intégrale,"* an integral, global, or total experience of one's own personal and concrete enduring in existence, apprehended in the process of intuitive identification. The outcome of this "life experience" is, first, the rejection of the pseudo-existence of the practical man who lost himself in the web of pragmatic reason and profitable action. Second, it is the process of transcending the state of self-estrangement and self-deception by exploring all the qualitative characteristics of personal existence imbedded in the process of a creative evolution. This process of self-transcendence should lead to the authentic and original form of existence.

Self-transcendence should be regarded as the transition from the mere physical condition of useful life to the region of meta-physical, spiritual life. Metaphysics, however, should not be interpreted again as the supreme science of being thus perpetuating the error of the intellectualists. Metaphysics—if possible at all—should still move within the interiority or inwardness of personal existence, which may or may not provide an opening for the descriptive analysis of an Absolute Existence.

The new philosophy of the existentialists appears to be a personal experience of the concrete existent engaged in the process of a live, dynamic, progressive transition from the lower levels of existence to the higher profiles and horizons of "authentic" experience. We shall describe in more detail the situation or condition of the free existent in the following chapter. However, here we may add, by way of a final conclusion, an attempt at a descriptive definition of existentialism: it is the philosophy of human unrest and life insofar as it involves the process of transcendence from the state of self-estrangement and self-deception to the experience of authentic life which stands for the revelation of the ultimate meaning of existing.

THE PROBLEMS OF EXISTENCE
MAN IN THE WORLD

The new philosophy of life tends to be the descriptive analysis of individual existence; which is experienced in the depths of introspective, integral, and intuitive self-scrutiny, since one is thrown into a hostile world constituting the natural *habitat* for the "human condition" or situation. It appears, therefore, as a mere tautology to emphasize that "existence" is *the* problem, in fact, the only problem of "existentialism." Yet existential philosophers do not spare time and energy to stress and overstress the limitation of the philosopher's concern with the boundaries of human life as the exclusively legitimate and worthwhile problems of philosophizing. Furthermore, while restricted only to the field of human existence, existentialists impose more specific qualifications. Indeed, in speaking of existence, they refer to the individual; that is, the concrete, singular, and personal experiences of one existent. In such a way they hope to preclude the methods of any traditional attempt at interpreting the problem of existence either in terms of scientific positivism or of the academic, systematic philosophy of the Aristotelian or Hegelian tradition. The new approach is a psychological (an individual case study) rather than a speculative and abstract discussion on the "category" of universal being. Consequently, philosophy is made identical with the act of philosophizing on a "do-it-yourself" basis because its proper subject matter is the sum total of subjective experiences in the constant duration and flux of change and becoming.

The individual experience of life as concrete duration discloses certain peculiar characteristics which make up the structural elements belonging to one's existential situation. There is first the experience of freedom, which opens future possibilities in becoming and transcending the preceding stages of existence. These future possibilities should be met with one's courageous exercise of choice, preference, and decision. Through these the existent will dispose or predispose of his lot via the act of projecting himself into the open possibilities of a future profile of existence. This heroic act of throwing oneself into the future generates the experience of anguish, dread, and concern. This self-projection is aimed at the transfiguration or clarification of existence on higher and higher levels of self-appropriation.

While the individual experiences his existence as challenge or demand for becoming he also becomes aware of his condition of being immersed or surrounded by the "world of things and objects" to which he finds himself related and bound in many ways. "Being-in-the-world" reveals, therefore, the second dimension of individual existence, radically opposed to the first dimension of personal freedom and indeterminateness. This new dimension stands for "*logos*" which is the intellectual, rational, reasonable, and practical concern of man dedicated to the domination of the material world (matter, time, space and energy) , directed at the provision and assurance of material benefits and securities. However, this pragmatic concern, demanded by man's practical reason (*logos*) , is antagonistic toward the free, courageous, even dangerous projections of the "*bios*," life, which demands spontaneous and creative evolution. Since both "*logos*" and "*bios*" belong to the individual's existential situation he will experience the outcomes of his antithetic constitution in the form of existential unrest, anxiety, and concern. Man caught in this conflict calls upon the heroic task to ensure, by constant conation and personal effort, the final victory of the "*bios*" over the "*logos.*" Thus he achieves the condition of an "authentic" existence radically different from the condition of self-deception, that is, self-estrangement of the "*homo faber,*" of the man dominated by the utilitarian concerns dictated by practical "*logos.*" Existentialism appears, therefore, as the new philosophy of life which, instead of presenting academic and systematic doctrines or abstract principles about the destiny of man conceived as a definition or generalization, calls upon the individual to change his way of life by transcending the logico-mechanical enslavement of existence through a constant process of striving for his true identity as a free, spiritual existent. In order to apprehend the meaning of this call, let us analyze in more detail the description of the two forms of existence, the pragmatic and the authentic.

Existence is the negation of non-being just as actual being is opposed to non-existence. To exist, therefore, means to stand outside of one's causes or outside nothingness. Something is the emergence of being from nothing; it posits the gap between being and not-being. Moreover, existence is first given as an experience, for nothingness never falls under man's factual experience. (It may be directly experienced as a threat of annihilation, thus generating the emotions of anxiety, concern, and dread). Beyond the fact of existing there arises the personal question related to the "how" and "what for" of existing. This question opens the possibility for a new conflict between inauthentic and authentic forms of existence, both related as a "no" or a "yes" to the "how to be" in order to make it worthy of man's efforts. It is exactly at this point where the analysis of the existentialists starts.

"Being-in-the-world" gives instances of different forms of life. The animal, for example, enjoys a "secure" life insofar as it is by nature "closed in," and well protected by the mechanisms of life-adjustment on the instinctual level. Because of this "natural" condition the animal is a satisfied being: there is no inner tension or rupture in the animal. The price of this safety and security is the inferiority and poverty of the brute as a mute, silent, but satisfied existence.

Man, on the contrary, is an "insecure" existent, being under the constant tension created by the bio-spiritual conflict immanent in his constitution. Man finds himself in the situation of "suspense"; that is, being torn apart by the polarity of his psycho-somatic nature, each part demanding the satisfaction of related needs and wants without a final equilibrium ever to be achieved. It is a condition of unbalance, unrest, anguish, and ambivalence.

Man is the only being who has to justify himself before himself and others. Beings other than man (objects and things) just are. That is sufficient justification for their being. They are what they are without the possibility of becoming something else (a being they are not as yet). Since there is no opening for transcendence in the mode of being of objects or things, their existence is once and for all justified by what they are. And they are always going to be what they have been. A stone, a plant, an animal is simply a stone, a plant, or an animal. They are just beings in their frozen staticity. Objects are never supposed to become something else. There is no "ought to be" in their existence. Properly speaking they do not exist; they just are.

Man is a subject. Subjectivity implies consciousness. Consciousness on a higher level becomes self-consciousness. Self-consciousness leads to the awareness of self-identity and the experience of freedom. Freedom involves the possibility for transcendence. Transcendence means the possibility of becoming other and more authentic than one is. While objects and things are closed in and within their pure passive inertia and staticity, and thoroughly determined by the rigidity of their physical constitution, man may experience, on a higher level of self-appropriation and integration, the insight into his real situation: as a free existent he is nothing definite and finished. In this sense, he is not: he constantly comes to be. Thus becoming fits man's existence better than mere being. In this perspective of becoming, freedom as the opening for self-transcendence cannot be applied and restricted to the sphere of action alone. Freedom constitutes the metaphysical reality of man as the existent who is not just being in any form of mere and continued identity. Freedom as self-determination is the condition for man's self-projection into the future possibilities of higher experiences.

Man's free existence implies the negation of any definite determination. Man is not the being he was yesterday, and tomorrow he is not going to be the being which he represents today. Since his existence means constant self-transcendence, that is, the denial of what he is now in order to become that what he is not as yet, one may not reduce man to mere being such as objects, things, and the lower organisms.

The opening for becoming other than one is, made possible by the indeterminateness of existence, takes us over to the experience of change and evolution. The evolving man on the level of self-appropriation is not dominated by the necessity and regularity of the physical universe. Consequently, man is the privileged being who chooses the form, content, and direction of his evolution on the immaterial level, for better or worse. Moreover, man is that peculiar being who may choose his existence or reject it altogether. Since choice takes place in the form of self-determination (free choice instead of directedness), there is no reason as yet to forecast sunny skies or heavy storms. Man is the exclusive weathermaker in the field of his existence. Progress and decline, self-appropriation and self-deception have equal chances on the occasion of self-determination. Self-transcendence may involve the acquisition of more being in the form of self-enrichment if the choice happens to be meta-physically motivated. However, choice may also involve loss in being instead of gain, regression instead of progress, existential impoverishment instead of enrichment, self-deception instead of insight; the choice of being just a practical and smart *"homo faber"* instead of a free subject.

Since man chooses his existence and its form, he is held responsible for his choice. This responsibility is, at first, experienced in the form of self-justification before oneself. The process of self-justification is experienced in the prehension of one's existence as becoming and progressing toward higher levels of self-integration. It is the dialogue between the "I" and the "Self." The exercise of this important freedom and subsequent responsibility generates the feeling of "dreadful freedom." Responsibilities on the social dimension of existence represent only the coordination, organization, and articulation of inner responsibilities related to those of the other selves who may or may not find themselves in the same condition of becoming.

It is the existentialists' contention that not every individual human being arrives at the higher levels of authentic existence. In fact, the majority of people are and will stay on the level of a safe, secure, well-protected, and insured life, such as the condition of the *"homo faber"* dominated and directed by the postulates of pragmatic *"logos,"* (the practical intellect or the agent of useful action and life adjustment on the material level of civilization). Let us describe briefly the situation of self-estrangement of the active extrovert type of man.

Man's natural habitat, according to the plan of nature, is in the physical, material environment usually called the world-out-there. Thus man finds himself "in-the-world-out-there" as the result, or rather, the first intention and the highest achievement of nature engaged in the process of creative evolution. Moreover, man as a natural product of nature appears to be an intelligent individual and a social being as well (*homo sapiens et homo gregarius*). Unlike the brute, well-protected by the mechanism of his instinctual behavior, the intelligent being must protect himself by producing or creating a safe environment which guarantees his survival and well-being. To achieve his vital demand of life man uses his intelligence as the power of anticipation, prevision in the constant process of his need satisfactions. Human intelligence appears, therefore, as a practical instrument, produced by nature for the domination, utilization, and control of man's physical environment.

The practical results of the intellect's inventiveness can be seen in the progress of material civilization understood as the sum total of the "securities" the *"homo faber"* fabricates while facing the challenges coming to him from his physical environment. Man's "securities" are of three kinds: 1) common sense and science, 2) morality of conformity, and 3) primitive forms of religious experiences. The existentialists undertake a detailed analysis of these securities in order to understand the "natural" locus of man according to the plan of nature. This understanding will then be used as a negative instance to illustrate a form of life which is the denial of the original, superior, and authentic form of free existence. Their preconceived ideas about the nature of human intelligence (as a practical instrument of the *"homo faber"*), are responsible for the unilateral interpretations of man's so called "securities."

1. Man's first security on the level of material life is provided by his intellect, described by *Bergson* as a "mathematical function of the spirit." This function of the spirit produces science and technology, regarded as the theoretical and practical guiding system, which are needed and utilized by man in the pursuit of his useful securities. Pure mathematics, mechanics, physics, chemistry, and biology are the landmarks of the progressive evolution of man's civilization on the material level.

Along with his achievements in the field of the positive and natural sciences, man's general intelligence is responsible for the origin, development, and functioning of human articulation. Language is simply another practical instrument facilitating the common action, cooperation and teamwork of the many engaged in the attainment of the common good. Active cooperation, however, presupposes the art of communication through which the many will be systematically organized and coordinated. Human language as the system of conventional symbolism is that useful device which guarantees the success of common action and effort through communication. Even the logical, dialectical, and argumentative processes of language should be viewed from this empirical and positive angle. They represent only a more skilled, more complex, and more efficient (more economic) method subordinated to the easy and simple achievements of the *homo faber*.

The anti-intellectual philosophers believe that the fundamental error of traditional philosophies (Aristotelian, empirical, and idealistic) lies in the wrong assumption as to the first and original nature and role of human intelligence. Instead of restricting its meaning to the practical ends of efficient activity on the material level, they believed that human language, concepts, judgments, and reasoning processes would truly translate the real "essences" of things designated by them. Because of this illusion they attempted in vain to construct a metaphysics or a philosophy which would reveal the ultimate meaning of life and existence. They failed to realize that the elements of human language and thinking (concepts, judgments, and principles) were only mere symbols; practical signs or directives for the concerns of the nature-bound animal. This basic misconception can also explain the abstract, theoretical, rational, and intellectual character of their philosophical doctrines, systems, and academic, rather dogmatic attitudes. On the other hand, their wrong conception of the nature of human intelligence necessarily led to the formulation of some odd principles, to the discussion of pseudo-problems and to the unfortunate multiplication of "systems." Each of these systems claimed for itself an absolute and final validity; the ultimate truth as the highest achievement of philosophizing. The contradiction between these academic philosophers and their systems stand as sufficient proof of their irrelevance. All this started with the belief that one can push forward from mere symbols to what is symbolized. The truth of the matter is, however, that the symbol never discloses the inner nature of what it signifies. At most the symbol may lead to the possession of an indirect, second-hand, and derived information about the practical aspect of a reality in space and time created by the organizing and systematizing activity of pragmatic intellect. The conclusion at which the existentialists arrive is the rejection of all intellectualistic and positivistic philosophies as being false. Human intelligence is only a practical instrument created by Nature; as such it is not fit for the art of philosophizing. As seen above, there is a new kind of knowledge, the intuitive grasp of original reality as concrete duration, which is the only legitimate road to philosophical experiences.

2. The ethics of conformity is man's second security. Its origin and justification lie in man's social condition as an integrated member of a well organized and well controlled society. Although the human being is nature's last and highest intention, Nature is still more concerned with the many than the one individual existent. (*"La nature se préoccupe plutôt de la société que de l'individu."* Nature takes care rather of (the) society than of the individual, says Bergson). The individual is just a cell in the social organism, without any personal autonomy, or, for that matter, any right to claim such free emancipation. In order to ensure that nature's preoccupation and preference for the social is not defeated by individualistic tendencies, the morality of con-

formity had to be created and enforced. It is the guardian of social equilibrium without which even the pragmatic intelligence could not produce the material securities for benefit of the many living in society.

Moral obligation is that categorical imperative dictated by nature through which the individual will conform to the common interests of social life. This obligation will dictate certain automatic reactions which will be performed by the individual agent who experiences the tremendous weight and pressure put upon him by the majority of the same society. Society exercises her control over the individual by imposing upon the individual the absolute must of obedience and adaptation. Therefore, society is the source, the rule, and the sanction of the individual's moral obligations. The goal to be achieved through this social hegemony is the continuity of social equilibrium and peace as the condition for material progress. Society also possesses the means to punish the individual rebel who dares to threaten and overthrow the common good and interests of the majority.

The social control system works through the medium of language which is now identified as *"la dépositaire de la pensée sociale"* (the depository of social thought). In fact, language constructs the system of regulation, prohibitions, proscriptions, laws, taboos, commandments, customs, mores, traditions, and ideals for good citizenship. It would be again erroneous (according to the existentialists) to attempt a discovery of a superior, perhaps metaphysical, meaning and value behind the rigid control system of social ethics. Its value is determined by its purpose which is purely pragmatic and material. Morality, therefore, has only an instrumental value; as the functional and expedient approach to the solution of social conflicts. The result of this social dictatorship (radical collectivism), is the enslavement of the individual human being and his complete depersonalization. Existentialists, of course, protest against this total subjection of the individual by the organized many. They demand a bold revolt against this state of affairs with a view to the emancipation and autonomy of the individual person.

3. What the social ethics of conformity cannot achieve in terms of social balance and peace through the domination and manipulation of the individual members, religion, as man's highest security, will do. Since science and social ethics are pragmatically motivated, they do not give the answers to all man's questions about the ultimate meaning of his existence. This shortcoming will be overcome by religious feelings, aspirations, compensations, and rituals. Its role, therefore, consists in supplying further securities attained by putting up as many mythical symbols and images as needed for the re-establishment of the equilibrium of the whole social organism. The belief in the supernatural, in the soul and its immortality, in supernatural rewards for the good ones and eternal punishment or condemnation for the evil ones, in the faith in God's omnipresence and omniscience by which He assists man in his everyday struggle for life and survival, are many examples of a religious experience or practice created by man's insecurities on the material level of organized social life. Religion appears, therefore, as the projection and anthropomorphic extrapolation of man's eternal and inner conflicts on a new dimension of supernatural and supersensory life.

The value to be ascribed to this form of religious experience is obviously prescribed by its inner finality. According to the philosophers of life, man's cultural and spiritual life is just a sublimation, that is, a functional mechanism of biophysical and psychic needs. Consequently, it does not reach beyond the horizon of an existence dominated by pragmatic postulates. It also follows its deficient character in interpreting the original meaning of the individual existence. Religion is, then, a social, biological, and cultural product conditional in its form and contents by geographic, ethnical, and historical factors. These are the reasons leading to the rejection of traditional ethics and religion by the existentialists. They regard them as simple securities of the *"homo faber."* As such they are useless devices for the authentic existence, say the existentialists.

The descriptive analysis of the kind of existence led by the *"homo faber"* is presented by the existentialists as an illustration for the condition of self-deception, self-estrangement, and forlornness to be blamed on the situations created by scientific rationalism, academic philosophy, and authoritarian morality and religion. The majority of their complaints and criticism go against the excessive scientific and collective organization of life and make individual emancipation and autonomy almost impossible. Modern man's existential condition in today's mass-society is depicted with dark shades and colors applied in a gloomy mood of overpowering pessimism which can be best identified as the symptoms of an overall crisis of life.

Modern man who is "aware of the immediate present" and "conscious to a superlative degree" in the phrase of C. G. Jung, stands again in the process of a new critical self-evaluation. He stands "on the very edge of the world, the abyss of the future before him, above him the heavens, below him the whole mankind, behind him history." His existence can truly be called "marginal" because of his cosmological, historical, cultural, and metaphysical situation. On the one hand, he stands as the climax of history, the final product of development in science, technology and organization; on the other hand, however, he appears to be looked upon as the "disappointment of the hopes and expectations of the previous ages."

Modern man becomes more and more unhistorical, estranged from himself and from his past, opposed to traditional values, and disloyal to his cultural heritage. He was looked upon as a possible destroyer of mankind in view of the catastrophic potentialities present in the latest achievements of science and technology. The experience of two world wars and the threat of a total self-destruction in the eventuality of a third one, account for the state of crisis, tensions, insecurities, dangers, anxieties, dreads, and despair which best describe modern man's state of mind. In view of this depressing perspective, modern man becomes skeptical about the absolute value or goodness and benefits of material civilization, of world politics and of social reforms. Every new achievement in the field of science and scientific organization of life adds to the danger potential of existence and survival. In such manner, the "securities" of practical reason appear to be no securities at all.

Modern skepticism is the sure symptom of man's estrangement from himself, from his fellow men, and from the world in which he lives. Being estranged, he is a solitary phenomenon amidst the crowd he is forced to live in and with. He does not possess the resources of traditional faith in himself, in others, and in the Supernatural, since they have been discredited by the last major devaluation of values in *Nietzsche*'s philosophy. Consequently, traditional values and their symbols have been discredited and rejected, while no new ideals have been created to replace the old ones to justify man's faith in the meaning of his existence. The substitute beliefs in the benefits and securities provided by scientific, technical, and social progress have been shattered by the tragical outcomes of modern national and international conflicts. Even religion no longer appeals to modern man as the answer to his state of critical dividedness. Religion too is classified as merely another traditional "thing of the outer world," without being the authentic expression of his inner psychic life and without providing the reassurance man needs for his acceptance of his existence as worthwhile and meaningful.

Present-day existentialism as a descriptive analysis of individual existence is the newest attempt at another transvaluation of human values. Most of the existentialist thinkers appear to be metaphysically motivated, at least at the start of their account on human existence. It will depend on the solution they give to the problem of transcendence as to whether their trial will lead to success or to another error with its even more tragical consequences.

THE PROBLEM OF COMMUNICATION
MAN AND FELLOW-MAN

For the existentialist thinkers reality is necessarily individual, original, and ever changing. This conception is radically opposed to the view of the positive scientists for whom reality is the sum total of universally valid laws which determine the course of present, past, and future events with absolute uniformity and validity. The existentialists also reject the logical necessities implied in the idea of transcendental panlogism of Hegel, which leaves no room for the freedom and self-determination of the individual existents. No wonder then if the philosophers of life point to the nature and characteristics of the individual form of existence, while dealing with the foundation and the justification for the problem of human communication.

In the existentialist mentality communication between man and fellow-man is a problem because of two reasons. First, there is the immanent character of insight achieved in the state of intuitive introspection. The state of individual and subjective immanence brings about the need and the difficulty to break through the circle of individual interiority of existence in order to reach and to communicate with the other existents, who also happen to be closed in the same inwardness of their introspective practices. Second, since human concepts and logical principles have been rejected as unfit for the communication of existential experiences, there is only one solution left. That is the use of indirect communication by means of analogy and dramatic staging of existential situations as illustrative, rather revelatory of the regions of individual existence. The understanding of this process imposes upon us the task of analyzing the psychological and ontic moments of individuality.

In the saying of *Boethius,* individuality is the state of being "undivided in itself and divided from anything else." "Being undivided" implies several qualities or perfections centered around that of ontological and psychological unity. Unity may suggest, therefore, harmony, symmetry, proportion, order, equilibrium and beauty. The human person as an "individual substance of rational nature" experiences the unity of his being in the conscious state of self-knowledge and self-identity manifested and lived in the state of direct interiority and awareness of one's self. This experience finds its more or less adequate expression when we refer to it as the mind, the Ego, the I, or the Self. The inwardness and unity of personal existence are, therefore, experienced on the level of individual self-consciousness.

On the other hand, individuality also represents the condition of "being divided from" other beings and existents. Thus "being divided from" involves two different sets of characteristics which further reveal the situation of the individual. First, it suggests the ideas of difference, dissimilarity, disparity, heterogeneity, and otherness. Being different from the others may further suggest the traits of singularity, originality, uniqueness, exclusiveness, and so on. Being unique in one's own kind implies the condition of loneliness: each unique individual finds himself alone with his own inimitable originality. The others are just different.

The qualities derived from the richness of individuality account for the familiar experience of incommunicability of existence in the sense that nobody has succeeded or will ever succeed in trying to share, transmit, communicate or give oneself in any direct form of complete communion, understood as the fusion, copenetration and identification of two individual existents. This fact further reinforces the condition of loneliness, for the barriers and frontiers of individuality will never disappear in any perfect dissolution of beings; there will still be the same one, even if added to the other, or better, there will still be two ones and not just one. In other words, direct communication between individual existents is not possible. I may give what I have in ideas, feelings, values, creations, and possessions, but I can not give away my own self. Therefore, human communication is only an indirect process. This limitation and frustration, however, becomes at the same time new sources for further trials and errors while attempting again and again the impossible, that is, the complete abolition and elimination of otherness, of strangeness, and of implicit loneliness.

"Being divided from" connotes, secondly, some negative aspects of individuality, such as, limitations, imperfections, unilaterality, and all the restrictions, deprivations and frustrations conditioned by them. The closed-in condition of the individual also creates the situation of isolation, separation, distance, and loneliness again. Many individuals may regret being only this without being that something else too. The amount of being and existence appears to be measured by ignoble hands allowing one to be only this much of being and not more, reaching only so far and not further, for being chained down only to this form of existence without being able to participate by identity in other forms, maybe more rewarding dimensions of existence. In other words, I am an individual only. As such, I can not trade in my present individual self-identity for a new one.

In this perspective, individuality is not a perfection or a blessing, but the source of unwanted limitations and imperfections. However, this "human condition" may create in some the need and the desire for self-transcendence, for becoming more, different, and better than one is. Under a metaphysical perspective this condition illustrates the disproportion between the relative being and the Absolute. In one word, the limitations in being of the individual existent creates the foundation and necessary conditions for communication. Its driving force lies in the desire for self-transcendence.

Communication as a quest for self-transcendence is directed first toward the other individuals who find themselves in the same condition of existential finiteness and contingency. Thus the orientation of the one toward the others is the first instance of self-transcendence. Only after the relative existent has met his equals, may he direct his desire for communication toward the Absolute, being still motivated by the same feeling of closed-in frustration. However, even in this last instance of self-transcendence, the road toward the Absolute leads first through the region of the relative beings from whom one derives the formal and goal-directed elements of the journey. At the same time, these relative beings impose their limitations and consequences. Since this is the case, the individual human being may try, as a last gigantic effort, a new, vertical, metaphysical move and jump over, above and beyond the horizon of relative existents into the region of the Unconditioned, Unlimited, and Absolute. On this level of experience communication becomes synonymous of revelation, mystical participation, and salvation. The one of the many becomes one with the Only One.

Our present concern, however, is with human communication among relative, individual, limited, and imperfect beings. Human communication is known in sociological jargon as "human relationships." It may involve the relationship of the one to a few or to many human subjects at the same time and place. Moreover, it may assume the form of universal and mutual dependence of everyone on everybody. This condition may be called impersonal organized mass communication through the use of the mass-media. Given its ever increasing complexity and the widening of its social horizons, it is opposed to the person to person, individual communication in its original, sincere and spontaneous form of friendship and love. It serves as an impressive illustration for the constant polarity and disproportion between the element of numerical quantity on one hand, and the element of quality on the other. An increase in quantity usually brings about a decrease of the qualitative excellence which may go along with only as much material as it can inform and shape into a meaningful structure.

It is our purpose to illustrate briefly the two opposite forms of human communication within the dynamic field of social interaction provided by both its quantitative and qualitative elements. Personal communication between individual members of a numerically limited inner group reveals the predominance of the qualitative element as its immanent life principle, directed at the realization and communication of true cultural values. The impersonal well organized, preestablished and technically controlled manipulation of human beings and their relationships on bigger and bigger scales, is subordinated to the economic and political interests of the many, more or less successfully managed by human engineers. The philosophers of life severely criticize and reject the manipulation of human beings as an instance of depersonalization and automation of human existence which leads to the condition of self-estrangement and self-deception practiced on a collective scale.

We identified above the reason for communication along with the limitations and imperfections of individuality. This takes care of the first question: Why communicate with each other? The other questions are more specific insofar as they refer to the contents, the channels, the purpose, the extent, the limitations, and the results of communication. These specific aspects can be formulated in questions, such as: What to communicate? What form or channel to choose for its effectiveness: What should be the goal of communication? To what extent should one go while seeking communication with his fellow men? How many individuals should be included in the process of communication without endangering its qualitative element, that is, the spontaneous and natural flow of human dialogue? What are the outcomes, the consequences of this process for the parties involved? While all these questions deserve the attention of anybody concerned with the problems of human communication, some of them rate higher in significance than others. It seems, however, that the problem dealing with the contents of communication demands our immediate consideration.

If the need for communication springs from the limitations of individuality, as an attempt at self-transcendence, it also follows that its contents should consist of the full range of human values that ought to be communicated, exchanged and participated in. This imposes further the obligation to proceed selectively, using the criterion of the relative excellence among human values and giving our preference first to those which rate qualitatively higher on an adequate hierarchy of values. At any rate, human values represent the backbone of civilization and culture. Consequently, communication between human persons can be justified only if it is value directed, axiological, and if it embraces the whole range of worthwhile values, without arbitrarily restricting the contents of communication to the mere economic, material, pragmatic, useful, sensuous, and pleasurable concerns of the needy organisms. Exchange of material goods and values is just one necessary aspect of human relationships, and is by no means the highest and the most important issue of human existence. Its maximum achievement consists in the ideals of technology, industry, and economy. While it takes care of the immediate organic needs of individuals and of groups of individuals, it does not and can not answer any of the more important problems of existence concerning the ultimate meaning, value, and transcendence of life. For this reason, one would hesitate to call it the manifestation of human ideals and endeavors, deserving rather the name of transaction or management of values on the material level of existence. These values are only contributory or secondary means for the achievement of man's higher aspirations. Should somebody design the structure and dynamics of human relationship only in terms of material goods, then this "organization" would not only defeat the purpose, but also prevent the possibility of true human communication.

The existentialists do not spare time and words in describing the deplorable condition of the individual forced to live in a state of absolute subordination to the condition of an atomized mass society, dominated almost exclusively by the ideals and interests of economy, politics and the implicit techniques of human manipulation. We live today in times of organized pursuit of useful interests in society designed according to the needs of the "homo faber." Consequently, human communication on a collective basis is designed for the many and is restricted to the level of exchanging views, opinions, interests, and information on the best methods for the accumulation and enjoyment of material values. Its primary concern is the guarantee of the continuous availability of consumer's goods, of securities which will provide the satisfaction of one's organic needs.

The visible results of this state of things can be described as a collective intellectual, emotional, behavioral, moral and cultural impoverishment. The range of human interests has been artificially restricted to the domain of the material as the organizing principle and driving force behind all social or human relationships. Human communication—if it deserves this title of nobility—becomes rather an unpleasant load than a wanted experience. It degenerates into the empty forms of public niceties.

The individual person living in the crowd of mass society is caught in the trap of an emotional conflict between his desire to emancipate, to regain his original freedom, independence and self-identity on the one hand, and his fear to lose his economic, social and political "securities." He may realize more and more his personal impotency to break away from the many and to be left alone for himself. In such a manner emerges the paradox of modern life: the individual is a solitary phenomenon in spite of being chained to the many and forced to live with him since he can not afford to walk out. There is an exaggerated emphasis put on the ideals of organized community life, social adjustment, social approval, cooperation and participation in public affairs. This emphasis, however, is already symptomatic of the lonely condition of the individual imbedded in the giant wheel of social dynamics.

The feeling of loneliness is conditioned by the very nature of the expanding collectivization of life. The organized human relationships of modern society move only on the level of impersonal formalities, of being just officially interested in others who happen to be thrown together in the same amorphous pool of life. The increasing numerical quantity precludes the way for personal communication on the cultural level. In one word, modern man is lost in society and at a loss without it. He is made dependent on the big organization in every possible form, but he is still left alone in the crowd to which he belongs.

The necessary subordination of the individual to the many is the source and the cause of many emotional reactions of the negative type. Latent hostility, resentment, feelings of frustration, fears, insecurities, states of anxiety and worries belong to the emotional make-up of individuals dominated by the supraindividual structure of social mechanics. The condition of helplessness may also bring about negativistic reactions in the individual, such as, apathy, inertness, impassibility, dullness, coldness, indifference, etc. In more active persons it may come to light in the form of discontentment, criticism, ironic, satiric, even sarcastic attitudes manifested both by behavior and speech.

The artificially forced integration of the individual in a mass society is a far cry from what one may call human communication. It may sound contradictory, but one may

53

describe it as impersonal human relationships due to the mechanization, automation, and systematic manipulation of human beings guided by the criteria of common usefulness. This mechanization is dominated by the ideals of functionality and expediency. It directs attention only on the general, average, mediocre, uniform, equal, and, last but not least, useful elements of civilized sociability.

Modern socialization of the individual results in impersonal human contacts of superficial impact because there are less and less strong individual persons with whom to communicate. There is no individual thinking, no meaningful philosophy of life above the level of practical hedonism, no ideas, no ideals, no historical consciousness, no national, ethnical or cultural unity. Similarly, cultural impoverishment brings about the absence of individual thinking, of true opinions, and of interests above the level of material profits. This leads to the state of mutual estrangement: one may not find mutual confidence, faith, and trust in others. The predominance of the economic concern makes man extremely egocentric, highly competitive and without scruples in choosing the means for the attainment of selfish wants. The condition of estrangement of man from his fellow-man transforms the traditional channels of human communication into superficial formalities or hobbies performed with a playground mentality. The pragmatic concern prevents the possibility for the establishment of true friendship and love. There is instead the nice and superficial friendliness well illustrated by mechanical smiles.

People do not have anything serious to talk about above the level of popular topics, strictly associated with the predominant pleasure principle. The modern individual becomes suspicious, inhibited, and even afraid of his fellow man. The Hobbesian state of *"homo homini lupus"*—man being wolf to his fellow-man—threatens to come back, at least in the form of mental and emotional tensions and hostilities. The overall inhibition of the individual reduces the number of questions one is allowed to ask. Most questions directed at the personal thinking and feeling of a person are not welcome; everybody is supposed to mind his own business. If questions are presented, evasive answers are given. Instead of definite commitments expressed in the form of a clear cut "yes" or "no," people carefully select a vocabulary dressed up with ambiguous, emotionally diluted, only hypothetical guessing with the permanent assumption of one being mistaken. The lack of courage to manifest one's straight opinion on a given subject is justified by pseudo arguments leading to the principles of subjectivism, and so called democratic tolerance.

If the condition of estrangement among individuals holds true, a similar attitude can be seen in the relationship of the individual citizen toward national and public affairs in general. There is no efficient participation or personal involvement of the individual citizen in the business of steering the destiny of his country. He became used to the fact that issues are decided at the higher places by specialists who are supposed to know their business. At the same time, however, the ideals of freedom and democracy are highly publicized by the mass-media without the individual person enjoying as a matter of fact the exercise of the freedom of thought, of speech, and of action. The control system of social sanctions, exercised by social approval or disapproval, prevents the possible emancipation of the individual from the state of universal conformity and passive receptivity.

The manipulators of human relationships are faced with an increasing numerical quantity of social units. Given this immensity of the material to be efficiently organized and controlled, they have to use a strictly statistical method and technique of conditioning. Collective conditioning is directed at the collective or social thinking, feeling, and motivation of the overt behavior of groups. While disregarding by necessity the qualitative differences of the individuals, they have to concentrate only on the practical means which

55

will render the functional, expedient manipulation an organized reality. Consequently, these "human engineers" use a relatively simple technique of mass conditioning which can be described as a useful set of do's and don'ts.

First of all, do not give the individual too much chance for individual thinking, choice and deliberation. If thinking is a must, directed thinking is safer and much more preferred than the independent critical evaluation of life. It is also good to keep the individual members busy, providing them with a busy professional and social schedule. Therefore, providing them with a process of pre-fabricated fun-process they will be followed by the majority. Individual tendencies and initiatives have to be discouraged because of their intrinsic danger potential. On the other hand, the standard of mediocrity and co-operative team work fit much better into the program of depersonalization of the individual. Moreover, the need for conformity can never be overstressed using the imperative of social formalities and emphasing the significance of the need for social approval. The ideal form of behavior should be presented as an attractive attitude of being nice and friendly.

Thinking ahead of the individual means presenting him with the ready-made solutions for any kind of problem he may have. Keep an abundant supply of the popular books which give well-tested advice on "How To" do whatever one is setting out to undertake. Even more efficient is the exploitation of the public's suggestibility by means of a constant appeal to his feelings, emotions, passions, and constant desire for happiness. Promise the guaranteed experience of collective happiness, a guarantee signed by the economists who will forecast neverending prosperity. It is good to keep collective ideals and slogans high so that the individual will not need personal ideals of his own. His consciousness of collective worth should take the place of the need for personal improvement and enrichment by means of personal communication.

Make sure also that his private life will not be any different from the reflex reaction he uses in his public relationships. Thus his tastes, his preferences and choices, even his most personal affairs, such as love and marriage, should become the concern of the millions, made public by the mass media of communication. In order to guarantee the success of human manipulation, it is most desirable that the process of conditioning start as early in life as possible. Accordingly, the education should be geared along the lines of average mediocrity and that of the pervasive pleasure principle. Education should be a fun-process brought about by making the process of learning a situation of happy adjustment with as little teaching and work as possible. This goal can be achieved by making all subjects of the school curricula look simple, easy, fun-promising, and popular: popular science, popular mechanics, popular music, popular teachers, popular hobbies, popular places to frequent, popular values which should be no different from popular drinks.

Finally, give the individual the illusion that he is the real cause of everything; the country is great because of him, and the future is bright. Do not let him develop, mature, and become his authentic self. In such wise the individual will feel important, great, and content, knowing that he has been accepted, wanted, well-adjusted, and his business is appreciated. Do not let him ever suspect that he has been made into an arrogant ignorant, a clown. Should he break down in the long run, put him under lock in a mental institution.

The existentialists rightly point out that mass-communication, or systematic manipulation of human beings, does not and can not achieve the goal of self-transcendence. On the contrary, it becomes the responsible cause of the complete depersonalization, disintegration, and self-estrangement of the individual human being. This situation imposes the need to reject the assumptions of mass-conditioning and to bring human communication back and up to the personal form of an "I—Thou" relationship, which will eventually lead to the satisfaction of man's higher aspirations for the immaterial, cultural, moral, and religious ideals of existence.

Personal exchange of cultural values should be guided by the highest category of perfection, embodied in the ideal of truth as the opposite of self-deception. Truth as the ideal of human communication should not be understood as an abstract category of science, of pure reason, of speculative philosophy, or of sheer theories about the meaning of existence and happy life. Truth should be the experience of persons leading the authentic form of existence, manifested by a superior degree of personal and historical consciousness which embraces all the dimensions of existence, both tragical and encouraging.

Truth lived as an individual experience and communicated with others, involves the values of understanding, intuitive insight, and revelation, effecting the coming of unity, harmony, order, union, and communion among human beings. Its final manifestation is the experience of love founded upon the community of human nature, the communication of human values, and the communion of authentic existences. Such ideals should be transparent in human speech which is inspired by true words, true ideals, true propositions, judgments, reasoning and conclusions. Human behavior should not be the ostentation of conventional formalities without any meaning to them. Instead of collective hypocrisy and misleading shows, one's behavior should be the sincere manifestation of one's true being. Similarly, man's cultural creativity, such as art, science, philosophy, and religion ought to be inspired and supported by the faithful observance of man's commitment to the conditions of his existence.

If cultural values are not degraded to the level of sheer interests and commodities, mere consumer's goods, individuality should not mean a permanent state of limitations but a process of continued self-transcendence aimed at the values of unity, goodness, and beauty on the scale of proportionate beings. Human communication as a form of existence could then be the process of a transition from the state of self-estrangement to the state of authentic existence, mediated by the insights into the perfections of being: unity, truth, goodness, and beauty; oneness without limitations; truth without self-deception, goodness without egocentric hypocrisy, and beauty without distortions.

THE PROBLEM OF TRANSCENDENCE
MAN AND GOD

Philosophy, unlike common sense and positive science, is metaphysically oriented insofar as the concern with the ultimate nature, meaning, and destiny of man in his world represents its primary subject matter and its formal object as well. Metaphysics, therefore, is the first philosophy which both etymologically and by real definition, implies the problem of transcendence as the passage or transition from the physical to the metaphysical, that is, from the phenomenal to the noumenal or original reality as the final answer to all the other questions any philosopher may ask. We arrive at the same conclusion if we call metaphysics the science of being—ontology—taken either as being in general or being in its transcendental structure and meaning. For being as such necessarily involves the problem of the One and the many in their causal or finalistic interrelationships.

In fact, the history of human thought, considered in its chronological and critico-systematic perspective, gives satisfactory evidence that any philosopher deserving this title of intellectual nobility and seriousness, had to face the problem of transcendence either in the affirmative or in the negative. Some of them, like Kant for instance, spent their lifetime inquiring into the a priori conditions for the possibility of metaphysics as such. The philosophers' conclusions may differ, as they actually do, because of the different assumptions or positions they assumed regarding the nature and the limitations of human knowledge applied to the inquiry of the reality of beings given on the sensory, intellectual, even intuitive levels of intentionality. Their differences on the success or failure of metaphysics, however, do not minimize the universality and the significance of the problem of transcendence.

The metaphysical or suprasensory concern of philosophy brings the philosopher to a close relationship also to the world of religious experiences, directed to the same region of otherworldliness, called the supernatural reality of God and His relationship to the "natural" being of the Cosmos. It has not always been easy for the philosophers to keep the metaphysical and supernatural apart because of the identity of their proper subject matter of inquiry, the Absolute. A very important part of the philosophers' effort was spent in trying to define the legitimate boundaries between faith (fides) and reason (ratio), supplemented, rather generated, by two different acts of the mind, the credo (I believe) and the intelligo (I understand), respectively. This shift in the emphasis put on the primary value of either believing or understanding justifies the emergence of empiricism, rationalism, intellectualism, transcendental idealism on the one hand, and fideism, intuitionism, and mysticism on the other.

The philosophy of life called existentialism does not and cannot keep itself apart from the problem of transcendence. Far from being indifferent toward the problem of a metaphysical reality, it has always been dedicated to this question. The evidence can be derived from both its brief history and the special language or terminology used in the formulation of the metaphysical problems. Indeed, S. Kierkegaard, whom we consider today as the father of modern existentialism—without including his forerunners St. Augustine and Pascal—was rather a theologian than a philosopher, trying to justify the validity of his faith by philosophical insights. Those who followed the new dimension in philosophizing by both faith and reason, that is, with one's whole soul as Plato put it, not only consider the problem of transcendence as one among the others which a philosopher should discuss academically, but far more as a personal problem and experience of the homo sapiens, of the authentic man.

Even a superficial glance at the "existential vocabulary" suffices to convince anyone of the most privileged place occupied by metaphysics and religion in present-day existentialism. Expressions such as: life, existence, suffering, death, states of unrest, care, concern, anguish and dread, freedom, decision, responsibility, fate, sin, and guilt; loneliness, forlornness, tragical self-estrangement, contingency, finitude, temporality, self-deception, shipwreck, revelation, mystical awareness, redemption through heroic self-sacrifice or the tragical fall into the fathomless abyss of nothingness, etc., etc., are among the most frequently used, sometimes misused and abused, expressions of the existentialists regardless of their optimistic or pessimistic attitude toward the reality or unreality of transcendence. This rather peculiar vocabulary also suggests the radically new approach and solution of the problem at hand. It is still this fluid terminology which makes any systematic presentation of their different positions on the problem of transcendence an almost impossible attempt. We shall try to succeed in this difficult undertaking by analyzing first the dimensions of transcendence to be followed by a description of the existentialists' metaphysical theory regarding the nature of that special knowledge through which one may arrive at that special experience which may disclose or reveal the reality of existence as such, along with the practical conclusions to be applied in the field of existential "acts" leading to authentic life.

Metaphysics is the road from immanence toward transcendence. Immanence, therefore, is the experiential foundation for the possibility of working one's way through and up in the direction of the suprasensory reality. The first dimension of this transcendental move is horizontal insofar as it has to imply the journey through the immanent forms of existence in order to find an opening for the second move in a vertical dimension as an ascension toward the Absolute. Accordingly, the philosopher must first give a descriptive account of the content present in the state of immanence in order to create a basis for a metaphysical theory of being and existence.

The first instance of immanence is given in the inwardness or interiority of personal existence. The philosopher may explore its contents in many different ways. The method of descriptive analysis may be purely empirical and quantitative, in which case the conclusions will be formulated as a mechanical and positivistic interpretation of immanence with the exclusion of any possibility for transcendence. Another approach may make use of man's rational or intellectual power for logical analysis while trying to determine the critical question about the possibilities of a metaphysical break away from immanence. This attempt may result in either the denial of metaphysics as the result of a thorough critique of pure reason (Kant) or in the hypostasization of man's dialectical powers by identifying it with the Logos, the Absolute Reason, the only reality acceptable by the transcendental idealists (Hegel). Finally, one may use the road of logical insights into the condition of participated beings on the scale of ascending perfections, thus arriving at the source of all analogous being, that is, the Unconditioned (Aristotle and the schoolmen).

The existentialists reject all the methods suggested above. As we mentioned before, their desire is no less than to reconstruct philosophy from its very foundations in order to overcome the positivistic, panlogistic, and intellectual falsifications of man's authentic existential condition. To attain the goals of this radical reform, the existentialists transfer the whole process of philosophizing to a "pre-logical," "pre-conceptual," "pre-judicial" and "neutral," that is, "meta-problematic" region of reality which they believe to have discovered by means of a new knowledge (intuition), leading to the discovery of a new reality (life as concrete duration and change), above and beyond the artificially created dualism of a subject-object relationship as the responsible element for logically structured reality of abstract essences. Let us now follow up in more detail the reconstruction of metaphysics from its very foundations after the existentialists' frame of mind.

Existential metaphysics is based upon the assumption that the proper locus and opening for transcendence is given in the form, condition and situation of the individual existence of the authentic man (homo sapiens) whose integral experiences will disclose, "reveal" the presence of the Absolute (*esse simpliciter*). The task of the philosopher, therefore, consists only in showing the manifestation of Being by communicating the contents of personal revelations received in the state of intuitive identity with the inner reality of becoming. Consequently, the new metaphysics is not a system of or a doctrine about logically demonstrated principles and truths; existentialism as philosophy is by identity the experience of the act of philosophizing. Philosophy is not; it is rather lived while leading the authentic form of personal existence.

The account the existentialist gives of his "pre-logical" and "metaproblematic" experiences can be best described as an empirico-phenomenological analysis and description of the human condition. It may be called also an empirico-phenomenological realism—a-theoretical and mystical—when referring to the experiences communicated by Kierkegaard, Bergson, G. Marcel and Jaspers. If the philosopher tries to submit an almost theoretical interpretation of his existential experiences, we may speak of an "existential ontology" or a theoretical and transcendental Existenz Philosophie (M. Heidegger and Sartre). As to the descriptive part of existential phenomenology, there seems to be some degree of agreement among existentialists concerning the new character of existential knowledge (intuition), existential reality (pure becoming and mutability), and existential actions (the efforts to maintain "authenticity" by fighting the dangers of self-deception and self-estrangement so true of the homo faber) . On the other hand, coming to the transcendental theory of existence, the disagreements outweigh the little amount of common beliefs in the possibility of reaching out into the region of "otherness." One may find both extreme attitudes, ranging from mystical participations to the nihilistic, pessimistic, and tragical conclusions about the meaningless, even absurd character of man's existential situation. It seems, therefore, more to the point to direct our attention to the phenomenological aspects of existentialism.

What are the experiences of the existentialist philosopher?

The inner structure of the original existence of the authentic man is experienced in the state of a new and profound form of inwardness, interiority, and pure intentionality, commonly designated as intuition. Intuition represents the condition of a total unity, identity, and co-penetration of the cognitive act, with its source (the person) and the known reality, achieved by the conjugated effort of thinking, feeling, prehending, and living the life of both subject and object in one global act of integral experience. It is the immanence of the whole being in the existent. This deep dimension of intentional communion with the intimate nature of reality can be achieved only by breaking through the superficial stratum of frozen objectivity and staticity into the profound reality of pure becoming. There are certain situations, such as the experience of personal conflict, crisis, loneliness, monotonous presence of "ennui" which condition the self to withdraw into the realm of his inner fluidity.

The states of inner recollection will reveal the essential qualities of existing. There is, first, the condition of passive receptivity of the person through which one comes across the fact of existing prior to any act of representation or logical reflection. One "finds" himself as already existing, an existence which imposes itself upon us as a weight, without having asked for it. Heidegger describes it as facticity, thrownness; G. Marcel puts it as "l'engagement à l'être"—being engaged in being.

The discovery of existence as a factual engagement in being, is followed by an active and spontaneous act of "understanding" the nature and meaning of this finding. At this point there emerges the experience of "freedom": though given, it is still "open" to an indefinite number of possibilities into which one may project himself by the exercise of his free choice and decision. Man experiences himself as the "master" of his existence insofar as it is upon him to decide the direction, form, contents, and meaning of the given. He does so by throwing himself into the future, understanding that his life, besides being given, also implies the demand for commitment. *("Das Dasein ist nicht gegeben, sondern aufgegeben"*—Heidegger.)

The discovery of "being engaged in being" implies immediately and originally also the discovery that I am not the only existent since my existence is already imbedded, almost immerged in the "world" of objects and other persons by a variety of relationships, attitudes, and bonds which determine the condition of my immediate profile of existence, my own existential situation. The ensemble of my situations is experienced as an original "being with" (co-esse), a condition of bondage nobody is able to eliminate. Furthermore, there is the imminent danger of self-deception in the form of following the innate tendencies of practical intellect which will direct my action toward the goal of creating the safe, secure, and rewarding condition of the homo faber in the form of a material civilization.

The danger of self-deception is averted by the experience of basic unrest and care for one's existence *(Sorge)* by which the authentic man protects himself against the temptation of losing himself in the world of objects. The intimate essence of the whole human existence discloses itself in the situation of anguish *(Angst)* which is the heightened, more intense form of concern and care *(Sorge)*. Anguish should be kept apart from fear which relates man only to a particular aspect of existence without involving the totality of existence in that overpowering emotional experience of anguish. Anguish translates and interprets faithfully the situation of profound crisis insofar as it reveals the state of absolute insecurity, impotency, helplessness, and overall dependence of my contingent being. Absolute contingency of existence leads over to the experience of nothingness, out of which emerges the dread before the perpetual threat of death. In such manner, I intuit the essence of my existence as being stretched over the abyss of nothingness and death: I am constantly headed toward the annihilation of my pure contingency. *(In der Welt zum Tode sein,* Heidegger.)

The experience of nothingness and facticity can be derived also from the insights into the original process of reality apprehended as pure becoming. Personal existence is thoroughly involved in the process of duration which, if adequately analyzed, suggests the condition of being suspended between two moments of nothingness: I am what I was, that is, nothing; I also am what I will be, that is, nothing again for past and future as such are located outside the horizon of actuality. This experience of anguish and dread, conditioned by the awareness of one's complete contingency, is of the greatest value to the existentialists, for they believe that it is here at this crucial moment of personal crisis that the "opening for transcendence" emerges. The emergence of self-transcendence may be described as follows:

In the state of a cognitive, affective, and volitive intuition, the existentialist becomes cognizant of his total contingency, dependency, and sustained existential agony. The thrownness of existence induces the feeling of existential responsibility; the authentic, responsible man should constantly oppose the instinctual tendency to get lost in the world of pragmatic interests and pleasurable distractions. With a serious and

66

tragic effort, the authentic man constantly strives for originality to be achieved by relentlessly projecting oneself into the future possibilities of a fuller existence on the higher levels of self-integration and self-appropriation. His profile of existence rises above the experiences of the common man and his securities; he is also superior to the condition of the scientist for knowing that true reality is basically different from the world of physical necessities and mechanical organization of life. His superior status applies also to the zone of philosophic insights, for the existentialist is convinced of possessing the original feeling of reality and life as pure intentional conation, and as such it is opposed to the logical, academic, and systematic falsification of existence. Finally, on the social level, he appears to be different for being inimical to the beliefs, opinions, traditions, customs, and everyday concerns and fears of the average man dominated by the need for conformity and uniformity.

While considering and observing the existentialist's heroic effort to achieve and maintain the values of self-awareness, self-identity, and authentic personal autonomy in the form of intensified self-transcendence and self-appropriation, there emerges spontaneously in the mind of the critical bystander a series of questions, such as: Why this enormous expenditure of vital energy? At what does the existentialist want to arrive as the final goal of his free projections into the possibilities of an unknown future? More specifically, what are the contents and the essential notes which can identify the achievement of the existential ideals besides the well-known states of tragical involvements in the process of concrete duration? Moreover, will the existentialist ever break through the narrow circle of his inner immanence and meet the Absolute Being in his complete otherness? These questions prepare the ground for a critical evaluation of the positive results of existentialism as the newest attempt at the radical reconstruction and rehabilitation of metaphysics.

To give a more or less adequate criticism of both the

positive achievements and failures of existential philosophy, we must go back to what they had promised to achieve as a solution for the accumulating crises and dilemmas of modern life.

The new philosophy of life, or existentialism, has been identified as the protest of Life against Reason. Reason has been made responsible for the universal crisis of the modern man and modern life. The crisis is the symptom of the overall alienation of man from himself, from his fellow man, from his world, and from his God. The onesided and excessive "rationalization" of life created a material civilization, designed after the pattern of a pragmatic and pleasurable want to create all sorts of securities for the average man. This resulted in scientific positivism and in a mechanical interpretation and organization of social life, hand in hand with the depersonalization of the individual human existent. On the other hand, academic philosophy came to a dead end, for the panlogistic systems of transcendental idealism had divorced themselves from living reality and the individual as the only carrier of existence. Consequently, traditional philosophy of intellectualism could not counterbalance the materialism produced by the advances made by technology and industrial development as the organizing agencies of modern life. The solution for this overall crisis seemed to be found within the symptoms of our socio-cultural maladies. Let us eliminate Reason as the responsible cause for the crisis of modern age.

Life (*bios*) as concrete duration was chosen as the substitute for *Logos*. Intuition as the co-penetration of the knowing self with its existence imbedded in the flux of universal life process, was supposed to eliminate the pseudo-formulation and solution of the problem of knowledge, of reality, of existence, of communication, and that of transcendence. The pre-logical, pre-conceptual and, therefore, anti-intellectual forms of knowledge were to create a meta-problematic situation in which the traditional questions about universal and abstract essences would lose any meaning and justification. Ontology with its primacy of being and essence, had to be discredited by the primacy of "esse," the simple act of existence without any essential objectivity to it. In one word, the old and traditional outlook on man (*animal rationale*), his world (a logically structured cosmos), his powers of knowledge (reason), and his hopes for metaphysical transcendence have been displaced by the new man (the existentialist), living in a new reality (life as concrete duration), endowed by a new power of knowledge (intuition) by which he hopes to arrive at the new reality of a new metaphysics as the dwelling place of a new God.

It has been our endeavor throughout these pages to give a legitimate insight into this new world of the new philosophers. It is time now to repeat once more the crucial question whether they have been successful in their attempt at a new break-through into the world of supra-sensory reality in a way that would satisfy the criteria of universal validity and objectivity. It is our opinion that this attempt, no matter how heroic in effort and impressing in its scope, resulted in a new period of trial and error. And the sincerity of the trial does not take away the tragical outcomes of the errors.

To begin with, existentialists have not overcome their opponents, that is, the idealists. The idealists' logical transcendentalism is replaced by an existential transcendentalism. "Pure reason" is opposed by "pure existence," interpreted as "pure intentionality" or "total intentionality" of the *élan vital*. Emphasizing only the formal element of existence, the existentialists automatically empty it of all objective intelligibility, thus committing the same error the idealists are guilty of on a different level of philosophizing. In fact, idealism disregards the existential order by reducing reality to a rigid system of universal concepts and logical essences as the outcome of "pura cogitatio." The existentialists, motivated by the desire to guarantee the primacy and priority of the individual existent, reduce the whole reality to an a-

69

logical, or pre-logical process of "pure mutability," succession, and duration. While describing this original reality of existence as the dynamic conation of the "bios," the existentialists deny all objectivity and objective intelligibility of reality. The dangers of subjectivism and relativism become real insofar as reality and life—for some existentialists at least —become completely irrational and absurd.

The same objections can be applied to the possibilities of reconstructing metaphysical reality on existential premises. Since the existentialists' doctrine on the "pure intentionality" of intuitive insights does not possess any criteria of objective representations, how can they arrive at truly metaphysical conceptions which should possess at least some degree of otherness? At least Heidegger and his followers (Sartre) remain faithful to their principles insofar as they deny the possibility of transcending the condition of pure immanence, of the absolute contingency and dependence of existence. For Heidegger, reality is totally circumscribed by the two poles of existence, that is, the Ego and his world. His "existential ontology" does not offer instances or openings for metaphysical experiences. Hence the pessimistic, nihilistic, and tragical solution of the human crisis.

The others (Kierkegaard, Bergson, Jaspers, and especially G. Marcel) are equally convinced of the impossibility of constructing metaphysics by the traditional tools of rationalism. However, they do not preclude the way to the Absolute altogether. They believe that the Absolute Being is present and He reveals Himself to the philosopher in his mystical experiences. While accepting the legitimate value of mysticism on its own ground, we may question its validity in the field of philosophy. What criteria can we use, for instance, to validate the emotional and volitive efforts of the existentialists to achieve the region of Absolute Being? These experiences being basically a-logical and metaproblematic, any logical insight into their objective validity is

70

made a priori impossible. The stain of subjectivism cannot be removed anyway.

We arrive, therefore, at our final conclusion by referring ourselves to the middle of the road attitude of moderate realism. Veritas stat in medio: truth and reality are duplex and not simplex. Just as *"Logos"* alone and by itself does not account for the whole of reality, similarly, the exclusive acceptance of *"Bios"* cannot embrace the whole region of physical and metaphysical reality. Reality is the co-penetration of *Logos* and *Bios* which is just another version on the old *Hylemorphistic* doctrine of the Stagira. Objective intentionality equally recognizes both the intellectual and logical structure of being (veritas entis, veritas mentis), without neglecting the legitimacy of the concrete singularity of the individual existence.

The combination of logical insights with intuitive awareness, may provide the basis for a descriptive analysis of human existence whose dimensions are both horizontal and vertical. The new synthesis would be truly bio-logical as the expression of man's ontological identity. This approach could also provide the ground for the solution of our present-day philosophic, ideological, cultural, political, and economic crisis on the national and international horizons of existence.

Metaphysics was described above as the road from immanence toward transcendence. This road is both logical and existential. It imposes the demand for a new re-evaluation of our ideals and principles, a new rehabilitation of values made possible only by the integration of the complementary elements belonging to man's existential antinomies. In such wise, the relative calls for the Absolute; the temporal for the Eternal; the limited for the Unlimited; the finite for the Infinite; the imperfect for the Perfect; the contingent for the Necessary; the material for the Immaterial and Spiritual; the purely rational for the intuitive and emotional; the scientific for the religious; the disproportional and disharmonious for the orderly and the beautiful. Power should be tamed by obedience; freedom by responsibilities; skepticism by faith; scientism by the humility of "learned ignorance"; progress by finalistic attitudes; radical socialism by a genuine respect for the human person's freedom and individuality; economic competition by social justice; material civilization by spiritually informed culture. Maybe in this perspective, existentialism could be accepted as a challenge for one changing his life, understanding that the new direction of the change—*la vita nuova*—should be metaphysically motivated.

PART TWO

FIVE EXISTENTIALIST THINKERS

SÖREN KIERKEGAARD

By Thomas Gallagher
Chestnut Hill College

If we wish to place Sören Kierkegaard in the history of thought, we should remember that he was not a philosopher, as was Aristotle, nor a theologian, as was Thomas Aquinas. He can best be described as an informal religious thinker after the manner of Pascal. For this reason, his doctrine will appear rather familiar, and will lack a certain shock value which is found in some current Existentialist literature. His message is simple. "Luther has ninety-five theses," he says, "I have only one. Christianity has not been made a reality."

We shall proceed to discuss, without criticism, his notion of indirect communication, the three stages and their interrelations, the esthetic stage and its deficiencies, the ethical stage and its deficiencies, and lastly, his doctrine on the religious stage and the existential thinker.

Any investigation of Kierkegaard's thought faces a double difficulty: one common, the other unique. The first is, of course, simply to understand what is presented. The second and unique difficulty is to determine if what is presented is presented as Kierkegaard's own thought or is a statement of an opposing position. The majority of his works did not appear under his own name, but under the name of a series of pseudonymous authors whom he created. Since he not only creates the stories and essays, but even their authors, he refers to himself as the "author of authors." These productions are generally classified as the aesthetic works, and their mode of presentation is called indirect communication on the existential dialectic. Thus, they are distinguished from works appearing under his name and employing a more direct mode of communication. (These are generally his religious writings).

These aesthetic works are important, and their pseudonymous authors are like so many postures which Kierkegaard assumes when speaking to us. Yet, the view of Kierkegaard cannot be said to be unqualifiedly the view of his authors. Why then was such a procedure adopted? Part of the answer lies in the relation between thought and action, as he understood it. It is this relationship which determines the mode of communication.

The relationship between thought and action is not one of identity. To anticipate an action in thought is still not to act. Not being identical, there is a certain bridge between them; and the transition from the land of thought to the land of action is made by an act of will or a leap. We could put it this way: thought is not the efficient course of action; yet action is the doing of what has been thought. Thought, though not action, is necessary for action.

Yet, some knowledge is more nearly related to action, to doing, than other types. Accidental knowledge is that kind which has no effect on human action. Essential knowledge is knowledge which is oriented to doing, to action. It is related to a person's subjectivity and to his existence as a moral being. If we take existence as meaning a moral existence, only ethical and ethico-religious knowledge have an essential relationship to the knower. Speculative knowledge then becomes accidental or non-essential.

Kierkegaard is interested only in essential knowledge; and his problem is: how can such essential knowledge be communicated? Essential knowledge cannot be communicated directly, for then we are still in the order of accidental knowledge which is not related to action. Ethics should not be taught as if it were geometry. Knowledge which involves action and subjectivity should not be communicated as so many sets of abstract and colorless propositions which seek only the assent of the intellect. Indirect communication has not as its object an impersonal assent to propositions, but a personal commitment involving the subject himself, which can more easily overflow into action. It seeks not so much an assent of the intellect as the assent of the will.

No doubt the indirect method of communication presupposes the knowledge of what is being communicated, or it presupposes direct communication. Its aim will not be to teach a system and add to the objective fund of knowledge. Its object is to stir to action, to vitalize truths already known, to terminate in a personal appropriation of what has hitherto been only superficially related to the ego. Kierkegaard recognized that the way is prepared for choice, that the heart is captured, only by an artistic mode of presentation, and this type of presentation is the method of indirect communication.

The early works of Kierkegaard then are the aesthetic works—characterized by indirect communication and the use of pseudonymous authors and personages. Each personage is an individual representative of a certain manner of existing and each one's manner is expressed in a concrete and psychological way by means of his conversations and introspective ramblings—not in pedantic and austere form. It is by becoming personally involved in these attitudes towards existence that Kierkegaard hopes to encourage the reader to make a decision—either this manner or that manner of existing for me. Indeed the communication is so indirect in these works that he does not even supply us with his choice. When the book is finished and the alternatives posited, the author of authors withdraws, and leaves to the individual himself his appropriation of a certain attitude.

Kierkegaard later repudiated the method of indirect communication and saw the need for a direct, apologetic, and unadorned witness to the truth. To provoke was no longer enough; he himself, under his own name, must become a witness, and it was under his own name that he criticized the Established Church. Thus, his religious works appear under his own name.

The chief burden of the aesthetic works was to present the doctrine of the three stages—the aesthetic, the ethical, and religious. The mode of presentation is indirect, and each stage is concretely verified or expounded by such pseudonymous authors and characters as Constantine Constantius, Johannes Climacus, Judge William and Johannes the Seducer.

In general, each of the three stages is a certain manner of human existence characterized by a certain attitude toward life and its purpose. Each of the three stages thus represents a definite philosophy of life, and each has its predominant interest and characteristics.

The first stage of manner of human existing is the aesthetic stage. Its focal point is pleasure; and the result of this pleasure, perdition.

The second stage is the ethical stage; its focal point is action, and the result of action which is victory.

The third and last stage is the religious stage. Its focal point is simply suffering.

According as our character is formed and determined by one of the above, we are respectively aesthetic, ethical or religious. The main intention of these early aesthetic works is not so much for us to enjoy the intellectual pleasures of classifying the various pseudonymous characters as aesthetic, ethical or religious personages, but for each reader to see where *he* belongs among the stages on life's way. The presentation of the stages is thus a sly education for the individual soul—and for Kierkegaard an education is a course we run through in order to catch up with ourselves.

Just a word about the relationships between the three stages.

1. Although it may be said that each of us is primarily in one of the three stages, elements of the other stages may also be present. In other words, the stages overlap and are not mutually exclusive in all respects. Thus, it is preferable to substitute sphere for stage and to speak about existence spheres. Spheres may overlap, but stages are always separate. For example, the religious person need not entirely leave the sphere of the ethical, break with it entirely. It is only demanded that his life basically point in a different direction.

2. Theoretically, the religious sphere incorporates the best elements to be found in the aesthetic and ethical spheres; the ethical sphere incorporates all the good found in the aesthetic sphere. The lower spheres of the aesthetic and ethical are not entirely superseded, but only dethroned, and all the best in them is kept.

3. Just as theoretically a higher sphere does not completely destroy but only dethrones a lower sphere and its predominant interest, so practically one does not have to pass through a lower sphere before arriving at a higher sphere. The three stages or spheres are not necessarily a curriculum all must pass through from youth to old age, but ways here and now of possessing one's self before the real. For one does not have to be an aesthete as the condition for becoming ethical.

4. Although the stages may overlap in the above sense, they are still distinct so that one is not simply the prolongation or full development of the other. However, for the aesthete, to progress as an aesthete he does not become ethical but only a better aesthete; again the prolongation of the ethical is still the ethical, not the religious. One stage is not transformed into another, but dethroned and the new sphere represents a new basic orientation.

This dethroning is not accomplished by the intellect but by an act of will—the willing of a new value to supplant the old one. Thus, one can be said to make a leap from one stage to another.

The first and lowest sphere of existence is the aesthetic sphere. This is the territory of the romantic and hedonist whose focal point in life is the enjoyment of the pleasurable good, irrespective of its moral value.

The method employed is unsystematic, and consists in analyzing the personalities of several historical and literary figures. Kierkegaard tries to enter into their very spirit and to reveal them from within. The aesthetes of history and literature comprise Nero, Romeo and Juliet, Heloise and Abelard, Don Juan, and Faust, for he represents the aesthetic personality in its culmination in despair.

The essence of the aesthetic view is the pursuit of the pleasurable in a primary and exclusive way. All aesthetes accept as axiomatic the imperative "live for pleasure," while for the educated aesthetes, those with more refined sensibilities, it becomes "satisfaction in life" and "enjoyment is to be sought in the development of a talent." This talent can be poetic, literary, or even philosophical.

As long as the guiding principle is that of "enjoy one's self," the aesthetic sphere is not transcended and it is unessential what the object of enjoyment is. The aesthete who happens to be a poet or an artist agrees in essential with the aesthete who happens to be a sportsman or a drunken reveller.

Judge William, in whose mouth is put the critique of aesthetic existence, wisely remarks that such a division or rather lack of it, is sure to be disconcerting to the more talented of aesthetes.

In seeking the pleasurable, the aesthete necessarily seeks the momentary and the immediate for only in the moment and in the immediate can pleasure be found. Since repose is found only in pleasure, and pleasure is not one thing or a lasting effect of one thing, to will pleasure is to will change and variety. In other words, the aesthete chooses only for the moment, and so chooses something the next moment. He loses himself in multiplicity. His life is fractured.

This accounts for the lack of perseverance and the oscillations to which life in the purely aesthetic sphere is exposed. The aesthete is not so much character—determined by himself—but a mood, determined by things over which he has no control. The major defect in such a character is that reason is sacrificed to the cultivation of feeling, and that the will, having been neglected, the power of decision and permanent resolution is almost non-existent.

Further, since the pleasurable moment is an uncertain moment, and even when present, not fully satisfying, the aesthete becomes a victim of boredom, ennui and restlessness.

The final stage is reached when reflection sets in and one sees the futility of trying to find satisfaction in the immediately pleasurable. If a new way of life is not found, the result is despair—a total despair of the personality and of life in general. Despair is thus the terminus of the aesthetic life, and it is found at the end only because it was unconsciously present at the beginning.

Lastly, many realities of life escape the sphere of aesthetic interest—evil, poverty, sickness, have no aesthetic interest. To ignore these, however, is to damage the full development of human personality.

The lesson which Kierkegaard wishes us to draw from his description of such a life is this: that a life, lived *only* according to aesthetic principles, is humanly intolerable to the individual himself and to the society of those around him.

The deficiencies inherent in aesthetic existence are cured by moving on to the ethical state which is that of duty. Kierkegaard has no written treatise on ethics as a distinct discipline, and has furnished no metaphysical basis of his own on which to rest his observations.

Since the Kantian ethic was predominant, Kierkegaard characterizes the ethical sphere as one where duty and obedience to duty are predominant. The standards in the ethical sphere are rooted somehow in God, and are not simply dictated by the mores of society. In fact, the ethical person may frequently be at odds with the prevailing mores.

Life is now separated from personal whim, and anchored in an objective norm which is possessed of absolute validity, and sets a standard which applies to all without exception. Those in the ethical sphere realize themselves by self-knowledge and self-mastery in accordance with this objective norm. The goal attained is freedom and steadiness instead of the despair and dissipation which characterize the life of the aesthete.

The supreme category for the aestheticist is the category of choosing *one's self*. To choose one-self apparently means to choose absolutely and in an unqualified way—to make a resolution at any price and without the foreboding of any upshots. What is chosen here is duty, and this choice is freedom for the ethicist. He is thus bound to perfect himself under all conditions by means of obedience to duty for he has chosen this in an unqualified or unlimited way.

In more technical terms, Kierkegaard regards the universal as a synonym for duty. The task of the individual is to realize duty or the universal (or the general). This universal or duty is what is required *of all;* it is what *all* should do. Yet the duty of each individual is not duty as such but this or that particular duty which applies to him in this instance. Such an application of the universal to the individual is another way of expressing the aim of the ethicist. Regarded in this light, the aim of life is to reveal itself as the unity of the universal and the particular. For example— the universal states that fathers should love their children—as applies to the individual, it means Abraham should love Isaac. The universal states man should marry; as applied, it means Kierkegaard should marry.

The fruits of the ethical way of life are easily told: it gives constancy and purpose to the individual, which is lacking in the aesthete; and promotes an open and guileless relationship between individuals without whose presence a genuine society of persons is impossible.

In his choice of the ideal realization of the ethical sphere, Kierkegaard seems to have been influenced by his experience with Regina Olsen. This realization—as put into the mouth of Judge William—is found in the state of "Christian marriage." The goal of the ethical life, its end and culmination in moral perfection is to be found in a happy married life.

Its advantage is two-fold: First, the emphasis on duty which marriage implies brings it into the ethical sphere and orientates one to an absolute standard which is not determined by the whim of the moment. Second, the sensual and romantic will not be lacking but transformed by resolution so that all that is beautiful and human in the aesthetic view of the relationship between the sexes will not be lost, but maintained. This preservation of aesthetic elements in marriage—but subservient to duty—constitutes the aesthetic validity of marriage.

Judge William describes the beauties and joys of married life in enthusiastic and descriptive and personal terms, which constitute a picture, and not so much an argument.

Marriage is a goal for free individuals, and it proposes a task which can be realized only by a resolution of the will. In the ethical sphere, this resolution is the most positive of resolutions and that which cultivates most thoroughly the individuality; every other acquaintanceship with life is superficial.

In short, marriage is the highest end of the individual human existence and the culmination of life in the ethical sphere.

Kierkegaard's main critique of the ethical view of life as self-sufficient is mainly found in the pseudonymous work *Fear and Trembling*. Such a view must be dethroned by the religious view which still will preserve all that is best in the ethical.

What must be preserved of the ethical is its devotion to duty and its emphasizing of the will which determines character. What must be dethroned is the fact that for the ethicist—according to Kierkegaard—duty is the highest absolute, and God Himself occupies a subordinate place.

The tendency in the ethical sphere is to separate duty or law from God, the source of duty. The outcome would be the identification of morality and religion. For the ethicist, God is just some force that imposes duty or law, and man's end consists in conforming to duty for duty's sake, not for the sake of the author of duty. In other terms, for the ethicist, the end of life is virtue, not a personal relationship with a transcendent principle.

The critique of the ethical view aims to show that virtue is not an end in itself, and that law cannot be conceived in independence from the author of law and as something self-sufficient. Law is not to be done away with, but only referred back to its source so that the relationship to law is determined by relationship to God, and not our relationship to God by relationship to law conceived as an independent absolute.

With this understanding of the ethical sphere, taken by itself, it cannot give a full report on human existence:

1. It cannot understand suffering and temporal unhappiness. When the performance of duty does not produce the happiness which it should, the ethical is powerless to explain it.

2. Its emphasis on the universal and general tends to suppress, in practice, one's individuality and one is led to adopt the mores of the crowd.

3. The ethicist, although exulting duty, gives us no *power* to perform it. The appeal to duty for its own sake is to abstract and remove from the weakness of individuals, to give a compelling and permanent nature to the life of the average man.

4. Most important of all, the ethical is unable to explain

the conduct of certain *exceptional* individuals. Kierkegaard's strongest case against the ethical view of life and its self-sufficient morality is based on his analysis of the so-called exception from the universal or the ethical.

The most prominent exception to the rule of the universal was Abraham in his relation to Isaac. Kierkegaard describes the trial and anguish of Abraham—how the Lord called to him and told him to take the son of his old age—his only begotten Isaac—for a holocaust; how the wood cut by Abraham was carried by Isaac himself, Abraham carrying the fire and the knife; how when Isaac asked where the victim was, Abraham replied that the Lord would provide one. How Abraham tied Isaac, laid him on the altar, and drew his knife for the sacrifice—and how at the last instant Isaac was spared.

According to Kierkegaard, the ethicist must regard Abraham as a murderer—at least in intention. Such a case transcends the ethical sphere and must be distinguished from the case of the tragic hero—who remains within the ethical.

Quite different is Brutus—whose son took part in a conspiracy against the state. The son was captured, and it fell upon Brutus to wield the sword of justice. Here we have two universals—a father must have his son, and a ruler must preserve the idea of the state. Brutus was both father and ruler, and, in executing his son, his duty to his son found expression in his higher duty to the state. Brutus still remained within the universal, and we are found with no paradox. The ethical as the universal is seen as the absolute with no end outside itself. Brutus simply expressed the universal by carrying out his duty to the state. Not to carry out this duty would be to sin. Thus, for the ethicist, to sin is to fail to carry out or realize the universal. Kierkegaard regards this view as not going beyond the categories of the Greeks and the pagans.

Abraham, now, is related ethically or universally to his son this way: a father must love his son (which is also to say that the father must not kill his son). This is as far as the ethicist can go. The ethical forbade him to draw his knife, and when he did so, Abraham became a murderer.

Accordingly, to really understand Abraham, we have need of a new category. In drawing the knife, Abraham performed a purely *personal* action and one which it is impossible to universalize—in fact, the universal forbade it. Yet, he was justified because he was in a private relationship with God. And it is this private and personal relationship with God that the purely ethical does not acknowledge. As Kierkegaard puts it, Abraham was in absolute relation to the absolute. Abraham's action was dictated not by the universal, but by the Deity Itself and Abraham acted not to realize the universal—duty of love for his son—but for God and as under His command. This situation Kierkegaard refers to as the theological suspension of the ethical. This does not mean that each of us may create his own ethics, and that there is no law for all. It is meant to counteract the contentions of the ethicists that duty or the universal is the absolute, and has no end outside itself. The theological suspension of the ethical means that God, not abstract duty or law, is really the absolute, and that the commands of the law are secondary to the commands of the law-giver. Or, in other words, the Lord is also Lord of the Sabbath.

Abraham is also singular in another respect. For the ethicist, what tempts a man is what keeps him from doing his duty, from fulfilling the universal. For Abraham, the ethical or universal itself was a temptation. To realize the universal would prevent him from accomplishing God's will.

The new category to which Abraham belongs is that of faith; he existed not in the ethical sphere, not as a murderer, but as a believer, as a knight of faith. The knight of faith becomes such because the individual is in an absolute relation to the absolute, here meaning God. He is justified not by the universal, but by this relationship. In Kierkegaardian terms, faith is a paradox, the paradox that the individual is higher than the universal, and the man of faith acts by virtue of the absurd, for it is absurd that the individual is higher than the universal.

This brings us to the third and supreme sphere of existence—the religious sphere. Entry into this sphere is accomplished just as entry from the aesthetic into the ethical was effected—by a leap or act of the will. This act of the will, however, takes the form of belief.

The ethical is not abolished, only dethroned and its commands may receive different applications by the religious person. To say that the ethical is dethroned is not to remove the binding force of law, but to subordinate the law to its author. Thus, the religious sphere can be characterized by saying that there is an absolute duty toward God, considered as Master of man and of the law or universal, as well.

Kierkegaard is convinced that such a passing over the ethical into a higher relationship will not lead to anarchy, for to be in such a relationship is the most terrible thing of all. It is characterized by a constant state of tension, to be constantly tried and in danger of slipping back into the universal.

The Knight of Faith is unintelligible to all others in the lower spheres, and cannot explain himself to them; he is more a witness than a teacher, and his own perplexity and isolation are his assurance that he is on the right road.

Moreover, one Knight of faith can render no aid to another. Either the individual becomes one by assuming the burden of paradox—fully and on his own responsibility—or he never becomes one. The responsibility and its paradox are the individuals alone—and there constitutes the greatness and terror of his mode of existence.

In paradoxical form, the absolute duty of one in the religious sphere is to give up duty (or the universal).

In spite of this intense drama in the interior man, the Knight of Faith presents the exterior appearance of the ordinary. He may appear "as a clerk who had lost his soul in an intricate system of bookkeeping—yet he does not do the least thing except by virtue of the absurd."

This religious sphere of existence finds its highest expression in Christianity, and Kierkegaard, in his religious writings, tries to develop the true meaning of Christianity, and how to become a genuine Christian in everyday life.

Without going into his religious themes or theology, it is possible to see that some of the characterizations of the religious mode of existence have a philosophical import. This is particularly true in regard to the theory of knowledge. Kierkegaard's theory of knowledge has two aspects: First, the thinker himself, and the kind of truth he is interested in; second, the reality itself which he seeks to know. First, as concerns the thinker himself and the kind of truth he seeks to know, Kierkegaard's primary division is between "abstract thought," also called "objective reflection," and "existential thinking," also called "subjective reflection."

An example of abstract thought would be the type of thought present in the modern sciences, as in physics and in mathematics. The movement of these sciences is away from the specifically human and free to the area of the impersonal and necessary. The truths which they attain are like bits of information which have no influence on the character or lines of the knowers. In brief, such knowledge does not affect the inner man.

Existential thinking or subjective reflection is concerned with one's supreme interest—as for example, the use of freedom, the meaning of existence for the individual and all the risks involved in just living.

It differs from objective thinking in that it includes an appropriation to one's life of what is known. Its end is not simply to know, but to incorporate one's life in what is known, to realize certain truths in one's attitudes and actions. In this sense, all existential thinking is subjective—

that is, it pertains to the religious and moral sphere and modifies the interior man. The exaltation of subjectivity is the realization that one must be inner directed and not outer directed. Thus, all existential knowledge must, in a sense, be edifying.

There is another important characteristic of existential thinking and existential truth—it is this—that it is practical, and not speculative. Its term is self-development and it is ordered or related to self-development. Existential thinking is not concerned with the truths by which we may live, viewed as so many abstract possibilities, but it is concerned with the truths which we live viewed as having immediate consequences in our daily lives. An example of a subjective thinker in pagan times was Socrates.

Secondly: What can be said about the reality which the objective or subjective thinker seeks to know?

As to the objective thinker, there is no problem. He seeks to know mathematical beings or the world of nature, or even man in his non-human aspects. Kierkegaard is not especially concerned with these objects.

His main concern lies in what should be the object of the existential thinker. Here, we must take Kierkegaard with his meaning of the terms and with all the vagueness with which he surrounds them.

The existential or subjective thinker seeks knowledge of *existing beings*. However, not all things truly exist. To exist, for Kierkegaard, is not simply to exercise an act of being, but has a more technical meaning, and is geared to his apologetical aims.

To exist, strictly speaking, implies two characteristics: change and freedom. That which truly exists has not only come to be, but it is constantly engaged in change or coming to be in different ways. Thus, existence can be properly applied only to the finite and temporal beings of our experience. God, viewed as an eternal and immutable being, since He is outside the order of change, will not exist in the above science. As Kierkegaard said—*God does not exist; He is.*

To exist is also to be free, to have charge of one's becoming, so what is of absolute necessity does not exist either, in this sense of the term. What has charge of one's becoming to be is obviously man—for he determines whether he shall act at all, or if he should act, or in what way he shall act. The existential thinker is thus interested in man, in free subjects, characterized by change and becoming. The existential is the contingent, the becoming and the free. In other terms, the existential is the historical.

How, asks Kierkegaard, is it possible to know the existential, that which is free? It cannot be known by the intellect alone according to some form of deduction, for one does not deduce a free action. If it is to be known at all, the manner of knowing the existential must be somehow in accord with the manner of being of the existential. Now the course of existential or free becoming is free will and so our knowledge of the existential should also involve free will. This means that the existential will be known by an act of belief which depends on the will.

This analysis seems to be far removed from belief in God, or any of the interests which characterize the religious sphere of existence. In fact, happiness, subjectivity and belief are inseparably joined in the religious sphere.

It is taken for granted that man seeks to transcend his environment, and even, his own person in search for something higher in which he can find rest and fulfillment.

It is also common knowledge that finite goods are not fully satisfying and that only an eternal and perfect goodness will complete man's transcendence. The only question is, does this goodness, or the being who is such goodness, *exist?* (In Kierkegaard's understanding of the term).

Yes, there is one unique case in which an eternal being who is goodness really exists, in the sense of being subject to change and the temporal. This unique event happened at the Incarnation, when God became man in the Person of Christ.

Here the immutable becomes a changing being, the immutable becomes temporal. God, who is, enters into the existential order in Christ. Thus, Kierkegaard refers to Christ as *"the existential."*

This unique event is also a historical event; it is not within any law of nature, but is the product of a free decision, thus it is an existential event and can only be known by belief—in this case, belief is termed faith. For this reason, Kierkegaard refers to Christ as "the historical."

In other words, assent to the actual fact of the Incarnation is not a matter of demonstration, but of faith—faith is not just speculative knowledge; it also involves the will, and so is referred to as a *passion.*

When Kierkegaard remarks that the *existence* of God cannot be demonstrated he simply expresses this doctrine in his own peculiar terminology and really means that the Incarnation is matter for belief and not simply for speculative demonstration.

This assent of faith makes the man of faith, and from this assent, there follows the Christian way of life which he details in his religious writings. The Christian is in the religious sphere—is a Knight of faith—where the individual is higher than the Universal.

From the point of view of the existing subject, such an assent results in the highest form of subjectivity or inwardness and existential thinking. The Christian is the existential thinker in the supreme degree.

In this way, Kierkegaard attempts to tie up the notions of man's happiness, his subjectivity or inwardness, his existential thinking and religion by saying that all these are given in their highest degree by an act of faith in the Incarnation and the personal appropriation of the truths taught by Christ.

Without evaluating all of Kierkegaard's insights and their

implications for a philosophy of knowledge and man (and most would involve serious qualifications), let us simply note that Abraham is not truly an exception to the universal which forbids murder. As Thomas Aquinas has it:

> God is Lord of death and life,
> for by His decree the sinful
> and righteous die. Hence he
> who at God's command kills an
> innocent man, does not sin, as
> neither does God whose behest
> he executes: indeed his obedience
> to God's commands is a proof that
> he fears Him.

Although this considerably weakens the case against life in the ethical sphere in that it shows that there is no incompatibility between a life of duty and personal relationship with the Almighty, Kierkegaard is right in insisting that duty is only justified by the absolute, and not by itself.

MARTIN HEIDEGGER

By Heinz Moenkemeyer

University of Pennsylvania

Martin Heidegger was born in the Black Forest (Southern Germany) in 1889. His father was a cooper, and Heidegger came from a family that had been settled in this part of the country for a long time. Heidegger always showed a deep-rooted attachment for his home, and for that reason stayed most of his life at the University of Freiburg, although he was repeatedly called to Berlin. After his retirement, he moved to a little house in the Black Forest.

Heidegger began to study Catholic theology and philosophy at Freiburg University, but very soon gave up theology to devote himself entirely to philosophy together with the study of mathematics and history. Heidegger's dissertation (1914) treated the relations between propositions and psychology, showing not only the influence of his teacher Rickert and the philosophy of values developed by Rickert and Windelband, but also the influence of Husserl's phenomenology. Heidegger's first book (1916), written to admit him to teaching at a university, dealt with a medieval thinker and was entitled *Duns Scotus' Doctrine of Categories and Meanings.* Heidegger already evinces in this early work a concern with Being, with the questions of the categories of being, and with truth transcending the "this-worldly" realm. In its center is the concept of the "living mind" (or Spirit), the subject in itself, which is of an essentially historical nature. Philosophy as detached from life is rejected.

In 1922 Heidegger became full professor at Marburg University and in 1928 at Freiburg, where he stayed until his retirement. Between 1916 and 1927 Heidegger did not write anything, but developed his own ideas in uninterrupted work. In the course of this work, he assimilated the thought of Kierkegaard, Augustin, Luther, and Pascal. Jaspers, with his concept of *Grenzsituation* (extreme human situation), and van Gogh's art were other influences. Heidegger is more familiar than most scholars are with the sources. After *Sein und Zeit*, he extended his interest to poets like Hölderlin, Rilke, Trakl, and, above all, to the Pre-Socratics—but never to the New Testament and Christ Jesus, despite his thoughts about a parousia of Being which suggest the Gospels.

The book which marks Heidegger's position within the history of contemporary existentialism is *Sein und Zeit* (Being and Time), which appeared in 1927 in volume VIII of the *Yearbook for Philosophical and Phenomenological Research*. This book was published as the first half of a larger undertaking which was to concern itself with the whole of Being, which Heidegger distinguishes as "transcendens" per se from the sum total of existing things, or concrete being *(Sein—Sein des Seienden)*. The last chapter of Part I and all of Part II are still unpublished, and probably will not be published, since Heidegger's thinking later took a much discussed and radical "turn" in which the emphasis was shifted from the analysis of human being *(Dasein)* to Being as such. On the other hand, it appears that the whole of Being was Heidegger's main concern from the very beginning, and that the full meaning of human being is revealed only if the whole of Being does not fade from our view.

After *Sein und Zeit,* Heidegger published in 1929 a book on *Kant and the Problem of Metaphysics* and a lecture entitled *What Is Metaphysics?* The former tries to interpret Kant as a forerunner of the thoughts developed by Heidegger in *Sein und Zeit,* while the latter concerns itself with the quest for Being as the proper subject of metaphysics, i.e.

ontology. This work appeared later in a very much enlarged version (1943, 1949).

In 1933 Heidegger became rector of the Freiburg University and wrote an essay on the situation of the German universities, expressing hopes for a regeneration of thinking from close contact with the historical situation of that time. His hopes, however, were soon disappointed, and Heidegger turned to an interpretation of Hölderlin's poetry. Hölderlin's (1770-1843) interpretation of our age as an age of dearth and lack *(dürftige Zeit)* and as the night of godlessness—as an age of transition and expectation in which the gods or God *no longer* speak to us, and in which the gods or God *not yet* revealed themselves in a *parousia*—exerted a decisive influence on Heidegger's thinking. According to Heidegger our time is the time of the gods that have fled and of the God Who is coming. It is the time of need; it exhibits a double lack and negation: the No-more of the gods that have fled and the Not-yet of the God Who is coming.

Hölderlin did not only influence Heidegger's analysis of our epoch as an age of lack and of "oblivion of Being," and Heidegger's eschatological—sometimes prophetical—vision of a decisive turn in human history sent to us by the gods or by Being. Hölderlin also, with his insistence on the themes of *Homecoming* (return to the Being and the gods) and of the *naming of the gods,* gave Heidegger a new conception of the mission of the poet and of the role of language. The poet, like the thinker, not necessarily the philosopher in the departmentalized meaning of the word, searches for the new meaning of the Eternal; is open to it as a "spiritual witness," and exposes the wound of time through his vicarious suffering and his vision of an unacknowledged dawn in the night of "oblivion of Being." In language, which seems to be "the most innocent of occupations" (Hölderlin), "we become a conversation"; we meet and produce a world, history, and destiny. Heidegger says: "Poetry is the act of establishing by and in the word." Hölderlin writes: "What is enduring is established by the poets." The speech, or "call of Being," finds its corresponding (co-responding) call or speech in the poet and thinker *(sprechen—entsprechen)*. Being speaks, and we bespeak it. Hölderlin and Heidegger are aware of the dangers lurking in the gift of language; but, in any case, from the time of his occupation with Hölderlin, Heidegger established a close connection between the poet as spokesman, guardian, and shepherd of Being. Like Hölderlin, Heidegger turned to the Greeks, predominantly the Pre-Socratic thinkers.

There is also a growing concern with language as such. *Sein und Zeit* showed already a peculiar terminology, growing almost entirely out of the German language and difficult to translate into English, with its vocabulary of mixed derivation. German and Greek build from autochthonous roots, anchored in concrete images and concepts, to which Heidegger, especially in his later writings, harks back in an etymologizing manner. This has encountered much criticism from philologists and from other philosophers who insist that valid thought must be transferable into other languages. According to Heidegger, however, language is not only a means of communication between people, not only denotative and referential, with an arbitrary connection, made by man, between the word-sign and the thing. Language is either revelation of Being or not. It arises out of the revelation and call of Being *(Zuspruch);* it masters man, who must co-respond and listen if he wants to be open to the "speech" of Being. According to this conception of language—which rejects the criteria of correct or not correct (equalling true or false in conventional language) and the operational criteria of verification of truth—the poet and thinker come very close *as far as they reveal Being* and rise above the language and thought designed to manipulate and to exploit nature and being things *(das Seiende)*. Essential is Heidegger's rediscovery that language and terminology are basic problems of thinking as such.

96

Heidegger's later writings move along the lines just indicated, concerning themselves with the questions of *Being* (1955), of *Truth* (1943, third edition 1954), and with *Plato's Doctrine of Truth* (With a Letter on Humanism). Indicative of Heidegger's "turn" to the problem of Being is, above all, his collection of essays entitled *Holzwege* (1950), i.e., paths, which suddenly become overgrown and end in the impenetrable. In this collection and in later essays dealing with interpretations of the Pre-Socratics, Nietzsche, Rilke, Hegel, Descartes, and with the problem of technology and the work of art, Heidegger no longer aims at a system and at results, but contents himself with the process of thinking which is toward the essence of Being.

Turning now to *Sein und Zeit,* we must consider the philosophical situation out of which this work arose. There were at that time in Germany four main philosophical movements:

(1) *Positivism:* with its rejection of metaphysics and a priori knowledge; its psychologistic approach to epistemology; its trust in the role of the analytical Intellect and in sciences; its pragmatistic ideal of knowledge as a tool. (Mach, Ostwald, Vaihinger).

(2) *Neo-Kantianism:* also rejecting metaphysics but maintaining the possibility of a priori knowledge. Like Positivism, Neo-Kantianism was mainly concerned with the principles underlying scientific thought, with epistemology, and with the methodology of natural and historical sciences. Basic problems were: (a) the analysis of consciousness (here, however, conceived in anti-psychologistic terms), (b) the analysis of the subject-object relation, and (c) the validity of values and a theory of values (The *Marburg School:* Cohen, Natorp, Cassirer; the *Southwest German School*: Windelband, Rickert. Both Natorp and Cassirer moved toward a wider concept of philosophy beyond the exclusive concern with logic and epistemology).

(3) The so-called *Lebensphilosophie:* a group of very dif-

ferent thinkers influenced by Dilthey, Nietzsche, and Bergson, who can themselves be reckoned among this group. Their common intent is to understand human life in its concreteness and complexity, in its creative agility. Life is understood as a stream, an élan. Philosophy must take account of life in all of its utterances, move closer to the concerns of life. This philosophy stresses the irrational character of life, setting up an antithesis between intellect and soul or life and existence. It renders a sharp criticism of science, and objects to restricting philosophy to epistemology and methodology and also to an investigation of consciousness only. Existentialism, especially Jaspers', shows affinities to this philosophy of concrete life as it is lived (Scheler).

(4) *Phenomenology:* Going back to Franz Brentano's (1838-1917) works on psychology, Husserl (1858-1938) becomes the founder of this school. His aim is to make philosophy an exact science by an analysis of the contents of our consciousness. These must be reduced to their *essence,* independent of their reference to the factual world, and then be analyzed. Consciousness is characterized by intention; it is always conscious of something, a directed consciousness. Husserl shows that every perception involves categorical acts, e.g.: *this* table *and* chair. The a priori is neither based in the subjective nor in the transcendental. Each field of objects has a priori. The laws of consciousness (e.g. in arithmetic) are considered to be independent from the psychophysical organization. Husserl's phenomenology is strongly anti-psychologistic. Scheler developed a theory of personal acts, intentional in quality, and shifted the emphasis from Kant and Descartes to Augustine and Pascal.

Scheler also proposed a *philosophical anthropology,* the task of which is to answer the questions: What is man's essence? Who is this being which understands Being? Scheler emphasizes the fact that man has become completely uncertain about his essence and being and knows it. The problem of Truth also needs a reappraisal, he submits.

Philosophic anthropology, however, did not avoid the danger of becoming a special science, a *synoptic knowledge of man,* making use of biology, psychology, and sociology. A *regional ontology of man* evolved, discussing man's place in the universe, but not asking what is it with man? or with Kierkegaard: Who is man (i.e. who can claim to be man?)?

In general, *Phenomenology* and *Lebensphilosophie* evinced a turn to the concrete, to things and Being; and, above all, a courage to embark upon metaphysics against a restriction to logic and epistemology. The central problem of metaphysics was no longer the subject-object relationship, nor the relation between mind (soul) and body, but that of *ontology,* the investigation of the being of being things. There was a turn from consciousness as a constructive, value-creating power to Being itself; from *constructive logic and dialectics, to the understanding of modes of being in analytic hermeneutics.*

Here Heidegger's work commences: The phenomenological reduction of the contents of consciousness, the pure intuition of their essences, leaves out of account the fact that this consciousness and its contents, our attitudes and acts, arise from and during the realization of our existence. The being of this concrete being is to be analyzed; ontology and philosophical anthropology are to be replaced by a fundamental ontology of human being *(Dasein).* The moments which can be shown as inherent in human being have not a relative, subjective, but a transcendental meaning. They make experience possible and are constitutive of it. Concepts such as care *(Sorge),* dread *(Angst),* and conscience *(Gewissen)* are not referring to our subjective experiencing of them, are not meant as anthropological descriptions. They are not to be taken as *existenziell* and *ontic,* but as *existenzial* and *ontological* categories.

What is revealed in the analysis of the contents of consciousness are not rational objects (Husserl), but human being in the process of existing, of realizing itself. Being is

99

revealed only in this existence; our being is in itself transcendent, i.e. transcending itself, standing out into Being, *ek-sistent*. This transcendence does not refer to noumenal objects outside of consciousness. There are no objects in that sense; therefore, the traditional epistemological questions (subject-object, reality of the outer world, etc.) do not arise. Metaphysics then, as ontology, grounded in an inspection of that which is revealed to us as phenomenon, cannot be attacked by epistemological scruples. The duality of subject-object is rejected; therefore, their conformity is no question. The single act of existence is the root for subject and object.

Man is essentially a being which understands Being, steps from out of Being to reveal it. Human being, the horizon against which Being becomes revealed, is never a datum, like an object. Therefore, Heidegger has always objected to an anthropological interpretation of his analysis of human being.

To work out the question of the *being of consciousness* and its intention is Heidegger's task. He asks for the meaning of Being as such *(Sein überhaupt)*; he inquires about the Being of being things (concrete being). The difference between *the Being of being things (Sein des Seienden)* and *being things* (concrete being—*Seiendes*) Heidegger calls the ontological difference. Being becomes understandable in human being. This must be analyzed. What is the essence of understanding of Being? What is the inner reason for the possibility of the understanding of Being? These questions are further steps in the quest which leads, finally, to the question: *What is the Being of human being? (Sein des Daseins)* Since this answer gives us the ground, the fundamental of Being, Heidegger speaks of *Fundamentalontologie*.

Human being, as already understanding and investigating Being, is (1) always singular, inexchangeable, individual; (2) always in relation to and concerned with its own being—existentiality. Analysis of human being becomes, therefore, analysis of the mode of being of *Existenz*, i.e. *Existenzial-Analytik*. The characteristics of human being found in this

Analytik are *Existenzialism,* i.e. not factually occurring human traits in the sense of anthropological philosophy, but *categories of human being, corresponding to the categories of being things* (Aristotle, Saint Thomas). To be sure, human being is always concrete, singular, inexchangeable—never the pure consciousness of Idealism and Husserl's Phenomenology; but the singularity is not meant in an empirical sense. It is a fundamental form, an a priori trait of human being.

Heidegger gives the *categories* of self, of human being. *Existenzial* must be differentiated from *Existenziell,* although the latter, as factual understanding, and decision or neglect and failure *(Versäumnis)* to make a decision is always involved. Heidegger does not try to construct a concrete idea (ideal) of factual existence and measure each against the other. *Therefore, his analysis starts with the indifferent, average, everyday mode of existence of human being.*

The formal structure of human being is *being-in-the-world.* "Being in" does not refer to a spatial mode of "being contained in," nor to a relation between two being things. It is not a category of things, objects; but an *Existenzial.* ("Being in" . . . is a verbal form corresponding to "I am." It means: living, dwelling, being at home with, being familiar with . . . the world.) "Being in" means to attend to, carry out, to take care of, etc. *(Besorgen),* circumspection *(Umsicht).* The world is not the totality of objects within it, not the factual world we live in. It is a connected pattern of meanings and references; a world for human being, with which it is familiar in an active, meaningful intercourse. The world of *Besorgen* is a world of material, stuff, and of work *(Zeugwelt, Werkwelt).* This world is a finite world with a horizon within which this world is disclosed.

Our being-in-the-world is constituted by "disclosedness." The world is not opposite us, but inseparable from us. We are always in the world. "Consciousness" is not isolated from the world of objects; there is no subject-object relation with all its problems in epistemology. Human being is not conceived as "consciousness," but as being-in-the-world. Therefore, human being is always transcendent, always *ek-sistent* into the world, overmounting itself *(Überstieg)*. This transcendence is *the basis for the intention of our consciousness,* always related to, directed to the world into which human being projects itself. The subject is no longer world-less, not isolated, because there are always "the others," another human being *(Dasein)*. World is world-in *(Mitwelt)*, and being-in is being-with *(Mitsein)*. Again, this is not in a factual sense, not *existenziell,* but *existenzial.* The intercourse with other human beings is not like that with things; not *Besorgen* und *Umsicht,* but *Fürsorge*: taking care of, heed, consideration, forebearance *(Rücksicht, Nachsicht)*. The isolated ego of Descartes' *Cogito, ergo sum,* the worldless consciousness with its desire to make the outside world certain is overcome. *One main aim of Heidegger is to go back beyond Cartesian dualism and its inherent abstractions and disregard for the concrete being of human being.*

How do we exist; what is our mode of being? In distinction from things, we *are not just present in space-time* (vorhanden). *We are concerned about our existence, about what becomes of us, about our self. The prefix ex in existence implies we are constantly outside and ahead of ourselves, projecting ourselves into our own possibilities. We are primarily and essentially possibilities of being.* This structure Heidegger calls *Existenz. Existenz* is the possibility of being or not being ourself ("Dasein ist nicht ein Vorhandenes das als Zugabe noch besitzt, etwas zu können, sondern es ist primär Möglichkeit." *Sein und Zeit,* page 143), i.e. of existing authentically or inauthentically *(eigentlich—uneigentlich)*. We either assume our own true, inexorable, changeable self, which cannot be lived vicariously, or we fall away from this authentic self which is our very own (singularity or inexchangeability being one of the characteristics of human being). *Existenz is the essence of man.*

But *Existenz* is only part of human being. Man is not mere

102

possibility, but *is* in his singular mode of existence, *thrown* into his *there (Da-sein)* and into the world. *Thrownness, being thrown (Geworfenheit),* is a characteristic of human being, indicating the fact that man's being-in-the-world exists without his having chosen either himself or the world. This thrownness is designated by the word *Faktizität* (factuality).

Factuality has to be integrated into *Existenz.* It means that we are assigned to the world and to our self and that we are answerable to them. We have to assume the "there" *(Da)* of "being-there" *(Da-Sein).* In Heidegger's later writings, man is a "throw of Being into *Existenz."* Factuality refers to necessity in traditional philosophy; *Existenz* to possibility or freedom (in which man refers himself to his own possibilities). Human being is indivisibly thrownness and free projection; in *Existenz* it is free over and above its own possibilities. Human being is simultaneously *thrown projection (geworfener Entwurf),* and thrownness, projecting itself *(entworfende Geworfenheit).* It is both necessity and freedom or possibility. Human being exists factually (thrown). *Human being, as related to being things, which it is not, and to the human being, which it is, reveals itself as finite.*

How are factuality and *Existenz* disclosed to us? (I do not touch here on the third *Existenzial,* speech or *Rede,* as distinct from listening and silence.)

(1) *Existenz* is disclosed in understanding, which reveals human being as a projection of a possibility of being, as concerned with its own, authentic possibilities.

(2) Factuality is disclosed in mood, in a "being tuned" *(Gestimmtsein),* or, as Heidegger calls it, *"Befindlichkeit."* One must not think here of a festive, elated mood or of a romantic mood; but, rather, of a pale "being-tuned" to the everyday, apparently empty, "being-out of-tune" boredom and ennui. In it we experience the dull, somber ineluctability of our being-in-the-world; the burden of being handed over to the world of being things; our being chained to the silent rock of being-there; our being thrown into a world.

103

As a radio tuner discloses the world of sound, "being-tuned," or mood, discloses the world, makes us aware of *how we are where we are.*" Mood, "being tuned," or *Befindlichkeit,* as a fundamental key which discloses the world, is an important insight of Heidegger's analysis of human being. There are moods and feelings which disclose concrete being overall *(das Seiende im ganzen),* e.g., 1) Genuine ennui, boredom, which makes all things and other human beings and myself fuse into a colorless indifference; 2) a state of not knowing how we feel or why we feel so; 3) a surrender to a feeling of unity with everything; 4) a joyful awareness of another human being, a "thou."

A distinguishing mood is, however, dread, anxiety *(Angst),* because it discloses overall concrete being and transcends all concrete being at the same time. *Dread is not fear of a definite object or event. Dread is fear of something indefinite and indefinable,* not related to any concrete object or event. After having experienced dread or anxiety we say, "It was really nothing." In dread, man hovers dizzily over the bottomless emptiness of nothing; all being disappears into the dreadful desolation of nothing. Man becomes "homeless" *(unheimlich).* We dread being-in-the-world itself and human being as the projection of possibility, as freedom from all concrete being. *Dread discloses factuality, thrownness, and Existenz with its freedom of projecting itself into authentic possibilities. Freedom is revealed as both being thrown and as thrownness at the same time.* (Kierkegaard has defined dread as a giddiness which seizes us when we become aware of our own freedom to make decisions and resolutions.) Dread discloses Being and Nothingness; discloses human being as Being held out into the Nothing. As Heidegger points out in *What Is Metaphysics?,* from this point the question of metaphysics arises: why is there Being and not, rather, Nothing? The Nothing is not reached by logic; it is only revealed in dread and ennui. Disclosure of the Nothing in turn reveals being as Being; Nothingness points to *das*

Seiende as the "absolute other" and to its strangeness *(Befremdlichkeit)*. The *thaumazein* (being amazed, wonderment) is given as the source of philosophy. Being *(das Seiende)* is transcended. If human being would not transcend, would not be held out into Nothingness, there would not be any relation *(sich verhalten)* toward being things, nor to its own being (as human being). From here arises the possibility of metaphysics as a quest for Being and for reason.

This genuine dread, however, happens only at rare moments. Mostly, the Nothing(ness) is hidden from us as we lose ourselves in concrete being (of things, etc.) and fall into the inauthentic. Human being is at first, and mostly, absorbed in taking care of everyday life (Kierkegaard's daily day, *daglig dagen*), shunning the freedom of *Existenz* and the abyss of dread. The self tries to hide from itself by making itself indistinguishable from others, following in thinking and decisions the general trend of what "one" thinks and does. I am absorbed by the *man* (by "people," "one"), the inauthentic anonymity. I get lost in the hustle and bustle, the "business" of life. Man is mostly in this most real state of being, i.e. fallen away into anonymity *(Verfallensein—*forfeiture). He may be absorbed in it all of his life; even if not, he is never really free from forfeiture, *Verfallensein*. No one can live in the sole concentration of being himself, for being-in-the-world means a temptation to forfeiture; and forfeiture soothes, alienates from authentic being, is caught in itself. Heidegger call this, *Absturz* (falling away from authenticity). Speech *(Rede)* becomes talk *(Gerede);* understanding becomes newsiness *(Neugier)* and ambivalence (duplicity, *Zweideutigkeit)*. We console ourselves (vanity fair of consolation—Rilke), speak, think, and are glad about things— even reflect on ourselves—like "the others." "Vanity Fair" is a symbol of human being, disappearing in the "average," in the "people." For Heidegger, differing from Rilke, the inauthentic is basic; the authentic existence is a modification of the inauthentic. Heidegger stays close to Pascal's analysis of the *condition humaine* and its emphasis upon the ever-prevailing tendency to dissipation. We forget Being in our concern with particular being. Later, this *Seinsvergessenheit,* this forgetfulness of Being, becomes a central point in Heidegger's critique of Western Man and his metaphysics.

Human being exists factually as thrown projection and as projecting being-thrown. It projects possibilities, but not beyond its factuality, which comprises also potentiality. Therefore men can say: *become what you are.* In this, the circular structure of human being is revealed. However, this is not a vicious circle; and the whole structure of human being is contained under the title *Sorge*—care, concern. I care what becomes of me, am concerned with self-realization. This self is rooted in the past, in its being thrown, in its being thus, in its factuality; becoming refers to the possibility of *Existenz.* Both imply the present, the absorption into every day concerns, i.e. forfeiture *(Verfallensein).*

Care *(Sorge)* has then three components: *Existenz* (future), factuality or facticity (past), and forfeiture (present). Its formula is: to be ahead of oneself in already being in the world, as being with the world *(Sichvorweg-sein im schon sein in [der Welt] als Sein bei [der Welt]).* This care is an *Existenzial* and has nothing to do with what we experience existentially *(existenziell)* as care, worry, and concern—with the ontic concept of *Sorge.* Now it becomes obvious why being with things was characterized as *Besorgen,* and being with other human being as Fürsorge, Sorge being the underlying ontologic *Existenzial*—Structure.

The being of human being is disclosed as *Sorge.* In *Sorge,* man's existence shows itself characterized as temporality *(Zeitlichkeit).* All three aspects of time form a unit at every moment in which future has a certain pre-eminence, constituting our freedom. In contrast to the infinite succession of instants in the world-time of physics, temporality is finite, has a horizon which, however, varies. Human existence (being), as a whole, extends between birth and death. Man's existence is historic, showing historicity in so far as he realizes time. Man does not have a history because things happen to him in time, but because his being is temporality. Löwith has pointed out the difficulties and problems which arise when one attempts to connect this historicity with "history" in the accepted sense of the word. Heidegger calls the three aspects of time its "ec-stasies because time is always out of itself, ec-static." Human being transcends itself always; it is ec-static.

Man exists first for his own sake and is concerned with his self; but, he is also concerned with other human being in *Für-Sorge.* Since man's deepest concern is to realize his authentic self, *Fürsorge,* on the authentic level, does not consist in relieving others of their needs or *Sorge,* but in helping them to become aware of their *Sorge* (i.e. to become authentic selves). Man becomes conscious of himself, discloses his self, only in Mitsein, being-with other human being.

If the preparatory analysis of human being was based on average, every-day inauthentic existence, the question arises now: Can there be any wholeness of human being, and how is authentic existence possible and disclosed?

Death is the impenetrable limit for the understanding projection of the possibility of human being. It is the ultimate and unsurpassable possibility; the most authentic, unrelated, certain, and, as such, indefinite possibility. Bringing myself before this possibility, in running forward to death at the ultimate possibility, (Rilke: "Sei allem Abschied voran . . ." Sonnets II, 13) my entire existence is anticipated (An illustration is found in Goethe's letter of 20 September, 1780 to Lavater, expressing resolve to build the pyramid of his existence). The flight before the dread of death is cowardice before dread. Dread of death, far from being objective fear, rather makes man free to seize his true possibility, to be quite himself. In everyday life, in the state of forfeiture of inauthentic existence, the fact that human being is being to death (*Sein zum Tode*) is shunned and covered up. Heidegger refers to Tolstoy's story "The Death of Ivan Ilyitsch," in which a man faces inevitable death which must be faced alone, which cannot be taken upon by anyone else. This man must tear himself away from all the tempting and soothing false comforts which we all know as: "not yet," "another time," "much later," "another one," "not I," until he reaches the basis of his hum-drum existence, and darkness is lightened with his free resolution to take death upon himself.

It is dread which starts the process of running forward to death as the most authentic, unsurpassable possibility of human being, and reveals Nothingness as well as possible freedom. Dread reveals the possibility of authentic existence. Besides this there is the appeal or "voice of conscience." Conscience is the voice of care *(Sorge)*, calling man out of forfeiture from his absorption in what "one" does and thinks, from his living from instant to instant, to the realization of his authentic self. "When man understands the call, he submits to his authentic possibility, *Existenz.*" Understanding this appeal means "to-have-conscience" *(Gewissenhabenwollen)*, as the possibility of being authentic *(das eigentliche Seinkönnen des Daseins)*. Conscience, as call of *Sorge*, discloses guilt and also indebtedness *(Schuld)*. Guilt is not to be taken in its special meaning of a moral state resulting from a moral fault; guilt in its use here is not that incurred by sinful actions. Human being as such is guilty in its facticity as well as in its *Existenz*. Being "thrown," man has no control over the basic ground of his being in the world and can never realize his authentic possibilities entirely. Negativity is unavoidable since man is "thrown projection" *(geworfener Entwurf)*. Freedom can be no more than voluntary acceptance and appropriation of "thrownness" *(Geworfenheit)*. Concerning *Existenz*, man, while projecting himself into some possibilities, must reject others; he can *not* choose to realize *all* possibilities and thus incurs a *debt (Schuld)*. Hence *Sorge* reveals negativity, the *not*. This means for Heidegger that man is guilty if guilt is the basic ground of a negativity, a *not,* inherent in and determining human being.

Guilt then is an irremovable debt to the self, conceived without reference to theology or any system of morals. Heidegger's conception corrects a widespread error that guilt is accidental. The call of *Sorge* to assume my authentic self means the call to assume my guilt. Conscience, calling man out of forfeiture to transcend its facticity, leads to the resolution to accept and assume the inalienable alien ground of my existence. Resolution, running forward, projecting itself, represents the possibility of human being to be authentic in the whole. This emphasis upon negativity is not to be taken in a nihilistic sense. Heidegger views human being from the whole of Being and is aware of its incompleteness. Nihilism on the contrary, is the oblivion of Being, the view of the world as mere object of man's consciousness and needs.

The meaning of *Sorge* is temporality with future as the primary and constitutive phenomenon. Human being is not just contained within world-time, but shapes itself into time *(zeitigt sich selbst)* by moving always towards itself *(Zukunft—auf sich zu kommen).* The past is always a moment within an integral present in memory *(Erinnern)* and repetition *(Wieder [herauf] holung).* The present is the moment and the situation in which man collects himself, chooses his authentic self (on the authentic level). Destiny in its true sense is only where death, guilt, conscience, freedom, and finitude dwell together in a resolution to make factuality wholly and radically one's own. Authenticity requires *honesty* and *courage.* There is no easy distinction between authentic and inauthentic as in Sartre, because the inauthentic is always with us. Although authenticity is an important and significant concept, authenticity in the face of my own death is only a grim and lonely triumph. What I choose authentically is an important aspect which is lost when authenticity of choice is made the sole end of *Existenz*. Kierkegaard, Marcel, and Berdyaev present Christian solutions, Sartre an atheistic solution to the problem of authentic choice.

Heidegger himself indicates after *Sein und Zeit* that the voice of conscience does not make man the center of Being. Man is a "throw" of being. Ek-sistence means standing out into the truth of Being. The seat of Truth is shifted into Being which reveals or conceals itself. Authentic man is the shepherd or guardian of Being and Truth. Truth and authenticity are sent by Being, just as true history is sent (*Geschichte—Geschick*). The greatest calamity of Western Man is his "oblivion of Being" which culminates in the will to will, a consequence of the nihilistic trend of occidental metaphysics with its dichotomy of subject-object, its ruthless exploitation of nature, and its forgetfulness of Being over the concern with being things. Occidental metaphysics kills God.

To treat Heidegger's later writing, I have neither time nor competence. I am inclined to scepticism concerning Heidegger's latter day ontology and his role as a prophet of Being. But I was decisively influenced by his analysis of human being, of the *condition humaine,* to speak with Pascal, even if Heidegger does reject such anthropological interpretations as missing his concern with ontology.

KARL JASPERS

EXISTENZ
AND
TRANSCENDENCE

By Donald A. Gallagher
Villanova University

Karl Jaspers was born in Oldenburg, Germany, in 1883. His father, a jurist, high constable, and a bank director in this northern town, was a man of cosmopolitan outlook and independent thought. His mother, with infinite love and indomitable spirit, Jaspers tells us, made her children's lives happy and bright, inspiring them with high ideals.

After completing his studies at the Gymnasium, Jaspers was matriculated for three semesters as a student of jurisprudence. Then he changed his mind and studied medicine. Receiving his M.D. in 1909, he worked as a voluntary assistant at the University of Heidelberg. In 1913 he habilitated himself as *Privatdozent* in psychology in the Philosophical Faculty and in 1921 became full professor of philosophy after declining offers of positions from the universities of Greifswald and Kiel.

In 1937 he was deprived of his professional status by the National-Socialist regime but was re-instated in 1945 at Heidelberg with the consent of the American occupation authorities. In 1948, he accepted a position at the University of Basel in Switzerland, where he still resides at the age of 78.

Personal relationships have always been deep and meaningful for Karl Jaspers. He was greatly influenced by his parents, family, and youthful associates. From his earliest years he yearned for personal communication with his fellows and perhaps as a result of this need, has always been grieved by the numerous and inescapable misunderstandings that beset men.

Among his teachers, Max Weber was, for Jaspers, the most important one. Weber conveyed the exciting sense of the possibility of really personal communion, as well as the mystery of existence. With Ernst Meyer, Jaspers enjoyed one of those rare friendships, the music of whose interior dialogue is uninterrupted even by long separation. Jaspers acknowledges as a genuine collaboration the encouragement and aid Meyer gave him in the making of his books.

Jaspers' wife, Gertrud, the sister of Ernst Meyer, was the closest participant in his undertaking. Their collaboration in philosophic pursuit, their communion in life itself recalls the intellectual and spiritual companionship of Jacques and Raïssa Maritain. Jaspers' wife was of Jewish origin and with her he suffered the agony of the Jewish people, and with her pondered ceaselessly the meaning of being a German in such a time where all over the country Nazi horrors were possible. On this problem he has stood firm, maintaining that the German people must face the question of their guilt; yet he defends, as well, the true German spirit and observes that the German ideals of intellectual freedom, pure research and culture as embodied in the German university have made a unique contribution to Western Civilization and will continue to do so.

Just as close personal associations have been forces in the making of his philosophy, so the philosophers of the past are for Jaspers not mere symbols of this or that "ism," or simply treasuries of ideas, but living personalities whose

112

presence inspires one's own search for wisdom and communication. For Jaspers, the history of philosophy must be grasped in a personal way, involving a thorough study of the texts but also the living in the philosopher's realm of the spirit. When the philosophers become, for the student, "companions of thought" through the ages, the real essence of the history of philosophy is understood as unique and irreplaceable, a self-development of the individual in communication with other individuals.

Jaspers found real sources of strength and wisdom in Plato, Plotinus and Saint Augustine, in Spinoza, whom he read at the age of seventeen, and in Hegel, but particularly Kant, who provided him with the principles that he took for his own. Jaspers lays hands upon Descartes, heralded as the Father of Modern Philosophy, yet these hands are not parricidal, for Descartes represented to him a thinker who threw off history and sought to lift himself from the nothingness of the "I think." From these, his special companions in thought, Jaspers was fortified and inspired to achieve his own aim—to restore the living past and thereby revitalize the present.

Jaspers can hardly over-estimate the significance of the recent philosophers Kierkegaard and Nietzsche. Their thinking, he tells us in *Reason and Existenz,* created a new atmosphere, shrinking from nothing and consuming as if by a gigantic conflagration everything stable and permanent. He saw that Kierkegaard created an otherworldly Christianity like a Nothingness, showing itself only in negation and in negative resolution; Nietzsche left "a vacuum out of which with its despairing violence, a new reality was to be born (the eternal return, and his corresponding dogmatics)." Penetrating their whole lives with the earnestness of philosophizing, in magnificence, they brought into being not a systematic position but a new and total intellectual attitude for modern man. Jaspers insists that no one can philosophize without taking them into account.

Of all the philosophers Jaspers knew personally, Max Weber was his Socrates (as Ernst Moritz Manasse puts it). This great compliment is a fit analogy. For Weber taught Jaspers that through all the barriers of time and space, in spite of the predicaments in which man finds himself, he can and should communicate in his quest for Transcendence. Even in foundering and the shipwreck of all effort, man comes close to the Transcendent, to 'Him.'

Jaspers was, for a long while, held back by a strange awe of philosophy and was also somewhat repelled by the formalism of so many professional philosophers. For this reason, he did not at the outset embark upon the career of philosophy, yet he was prompted to philosophize as soon as he began leading a serious intellectual life with the reading of Spinoza.

Before World War II, he attempted to present his thought systematically in three major works (with each of which were associated certain of his shorter books and studies). These are *Psychopathology, Psychology of Weltanschauungen,* and his monumental *Philosophie.*

In the *Psychopathology* he investigated methods of research to demonstrate what each method could yield. His purpose was liberation of psychiatrists from dogmatism and fortification of research by clear consciousness of methods and limitations. In this work Jaspers is, of course, writing as a psychopathologist, but Jaspers the philosopher may be already seen emerging.

In his *Psychology of Weltanschauungen,* he endeavors to present all the possible ways in which human beings may adhere to faith, hold world views and possess attitudes. He recognizes in this book "a hidden philosophy misunderstanding itself as objectively descriptive psychology" and considers it, in historical retrospect, as "the earliest writing in the later so-called Existentialism."

It is, of course, readily seen from his philosophical interests that Jaspers has always been opposed to "system" as

114

a totality in which being and truth are presented as though fixed in final form, yet at the same time he has always tried to be systematic in presenting his thought. It was in *Philosophie* that he proceeded to the first formal and methodological statement of his philosophy and its characteristic themes of Transcendence and Existenz.

In recent years Jaspers has been engaged upon two large-scale projects which he considers to be the concluding efforts of his life. One is a *Philosophical Logic* in which he seeks to contribute to the logical self-consciousness of the age. Some of his ideas have been expounded in lecture form in *Reason and Existenz*, and in *Existenz Philosophie*. The first part of the logic, *Von der Wahrheit* (a volume of over 1000 pages) has been published already.

The other project is a Universal History of Philosophy. Jaspers, as we have already seen, takes the work of his philosophical predecessors seriously; in his universal history he aims to present historical philosophizing as the one great phenomenon, coherent in itself, of the revelation of Being in humanity. He hopes to show how, from its roots in China, India and Greece, philosophy developed in great cycles, constantly conditioned by sociological circumstances and psychological events, striving toward a single great organized unity of opposites which, if they fail to yield solutions in time, will in failing, bring to awareness the truth of Transcendence.

Jaspers recognizes that his colossal task is super-human and beyond the powers of a single man, yet he believes the impossible has to be attempted, for a synthesis in one mind must somehow be attained. He feels he must endeavor to draw together the life-work of countless historians in the past and sketch at least a vast panorama which others may fill in.

Like the other "Existentialists," Karl Jaspers has not been an ostrich-philosopher, with head in the sand and tail feathers brushing the clouds. He has always been deeply concerned with man's situation in the present age (as have been Belloc, Dawson, Maritain and Marcel). Jaspers has always been alive to the anguish of our time (to paraphrase Maritain, and in the book by which he first became known to the general educated public, *Man in the Modern Age*, he provided in his turn an analysis of contemporary civilization.

The crisis in which we find ourselves today is expressed by Jaspers in these vigorous words:

> The unsheltered individual gives our epoch its physiognomy: in rebelliousness; in the despair of nihilism; in the perplexity of the multitude of persons who remain unfulfilled; in a search along false paths on the part of those who renounce finite goals and withstand harmonizing lures. 'There is no God' cry the masses more and more vociferously; and with the loss of his God, man loses his sense of values—is, as it were, massacred because he feels himself of no account.

In his analysis of the spiritual-intellectual climate of our time, Jaspers makes much use of one of the most fundamental notions of his philosophy, that of situation. But the *Grenzsituation,* or ultimate situation, refers to such unavoidable facts as the very inescapability of situation itself, of conflict, of guilt, of suffering, of death, all of which are incurred in the living of one's life. In one of his most important contributions to philosophy, Jaspers describes these ultimate or "boundary" situations with extraordinary penetration and phenomenological accuracy. (Although he is less dependent on phenomenology than certain other Existentialists, Jaspers acknowledges an indebtedness to some Husserlian methods, particularly in descriptive psychology). And it is in the notion of situation that the starting-point of philosophy, for Jaspers, may be ascertained.

There is, in Jaspers' thought, no simple answer to the

116

question of where to start philosophizing. For philosophy begins in loneliness, it begins in communication or in recognition of the need for it; it begins in the present moment in history and yet, it also starts with the companion-minds of the past who are living for us; it begins with experience in the situation in which we find ourselves.

The basic questions of philosophy grow from life experience, and since they correspond and keep current with man's situation, they are part of the historical situation as well. For this reason, questions asked earlier in history are, today, our questions—in part identical, in part distant so that they can be made totally our own only by means of translation.

Jaspers reminds his readers that Kant asked, with moving simplicity, four basic questions: 1. What can I know? 2. What shall I do? 3. What may I hope? 4. What is man? Today these same questions, rethought and reasked, must involve science, communication, truth, man, and Transcendence.

Jaspers, himself once a scientist, clearly sees the overwhelming role that this colossus plays in modern civilization. Greatly extended in our day, science makes the Kantian investigation of knowledge and Kant's question (what can I know?) more concrete, yet limitless, inexorable, and even threatening. For there is ever-present the danger that man will assume the facts of science to be truth itself, the ultimate in knowledge.

Science, in fact, plays its most important role in showing where philosophy must start. Knowledge of life's facticity increases mastery of what is knowable; because science has become so all-pervasive, forcing humanity to obey it or to perish, man acquires through facing it, intensified consciousness of the historical situation. This permits him to live fully—if not anxiously—in the spiritual climate of his time. A clarity of consciousness is reached only when man progresses through science, and then beyond it and its limitations and dogmatic views of the world, to the totality of the world

117

and its reality. Then there is freedom from the scientific superstition of omniscience; by free use of science, man becomes receptive to that which lies beyond science itself— a universal consciousness that illuminates Being itself.

However, the "over-coming" of science cannot be achieved in isolation. Man, in fact, cannot even become human in isolation.

The very regulation which science has imposed, the order it has wrought, gathers the individuals of the community of mass human beings into a technically functioning organization which, because it is external, of necessity does not touch the inwardness of man. This situation has brought forth loneliness that never before existed, a dissatisfaction with mere achievement, an emptiness that seeks a release and seems always to end in frustration. Because of this, man experiences the real need for communication, for in his loneliness, his foothold in life is swept away, his ultimates are gone, his moral laws appear invalid. No longer will the categorical imperative establish the foundation for living (whether the imperative is wrong or right). Kant's question, what shall I do? presupposes, today, communication in depth, for knowledge reaches its fullness only through the bond that such communication creates between man.

The limits of science, the urge to communication, both point to a truth that can never be a "possession" of the intellect. This truth makes itself felt at the boundaries of science; this truth makes itself felt in the movement of communication, for communication is the path to truth in all its forms. The intellect finds clarity only in discussion; man as an existent is and can be only in communication which allows all other truth to appear. We shall see how this occurs later in our discussion. For the present, Jaspers' own question asserts itself: what is this truth?

Man inquires after being; he encounters it in the objects of his experience and the horizons of his life or limits of his knowledge. Yet from these objects and horizons and limits, being recedes as though giving notification of its presence, and testifying that it cannot be restricted to any one facet of man's experience. This is the Encompassing— "that which always makes its presence known, which does not appear itself, but from which everything comes to us."

The truth for which science and communication reach and toward which they point has its source in the Encompassing. Thus the notion of the Encompassing is of cardinal importance for an understanding of the philosophy of Karl Jaspers. In it lies his way to wisdom. Yet it is such an all-engrossing, all-comprehending notion that an attempt to summarize it seems wellnigh impossible. For *thought* of the Encompassing is a purely formal concept. Its notes emerge only upon further elaboration, and in a somewhat roundabout fashion. It is as though one must creep up behind the Encompassing and quickly capture it before it can escape. Even then, it will likely slip away upon the next examination, only to appear again when least expected. For the Encompassing is not a horizon, enclosing the determinate modes of being and truth that man knows; it is, rather, that which encloses the horizons themselves.

This is the reason for the possibility of two opposed approaches to the Encompassing. One is the approach to Being *Itself*, in which and through which man is. In this most usual and natural way, Being is generally described as Nature, or World, or God. But the other approach is through the Encompassing that *man is*. And for Jaspers, this approach is unavoidable since the advent of Kantian philosophy.

Man is, first of all, empirical existence, knowledge of which may be had on physical, biological and psychological levels. The Encompassing which this physical existent is may not, however, be understood unless man is taken in a sense of the totality of his actuality, in which his particularities of matter, living body, and soul are not only included, but also cannot be separated. The Encompassing of the empirical existence of man is the whole of that man. Because of this, the scientist's claim to know man is meaningless, since science studies only the separate aspects of his being.

Consciousness can be the second mode of the Encompassing which man is. Only those things which man experiences have being for him; as a result, all things entering his awareness must appear under forms which his consciousness can assimilate. This, of course, leads man to limit the Encompassing, in his own mind, to that which is thinkable. Yet Jaspers stresses that once man is aware of the limitations of his experience, he at least becomes open to the possibility of the unknown. He then rises beyond his mere consciousness of objects and enters the realm of consciousness *as such*. In this way, his consciousness is his Encompassing.

> As the consciousness of living beings, we are split into the multiplicity of endless particular realities, imprisoned in the narrowness of the individual and not encompassing. As consciousness in general we participate in . . . the universally valid truth, and . . . are an infinite Encompassing. . . . We participate in the encompassing through the possibility of common knowledge of Being in every form in which it appears to consciousness.

Man's third mode of the Encompassing is Spirit. This is the concrete totality of his consciousness as such, of his individual intelligible thought, action, feeling, comprehensive reality. It is actualized by itself and by what it encounters in the world. As Spirit, man consciously relates himself to everything he comprehends and in this mode of the Encompassing he comes to know himself and his world as one, unique, all-embracing reality. Spirit is necessarily oriented to the truth of consciousness as such, as well as to the world it encounters. It is the process of fusing and reconstructing all totalities in a present which ever changes and is yet always fulfilled.

Since it pushes toward the whole, spirit would preserve, enhance, and relate everything to everything else, exclude nothing, and give to everything its place and limits.

These modes of the Encompassing are not three separate entities, but three starting points through which man approaches the being that he is. He lives in his world as an empirical existence; as consciousness he is oriented toward objects; as spirit, he shapes the idea of a whole in his world existence.

Where does this analysis of man lead? Only to the limits again, as in science, but this time with a clearer understanding of the horizon. For man's being is but an appearance in the Encompassing of Being—Being Itself lies beyond the limits. Being Itself is the Transcendence which is not evident in any investigation because it is always beyond; yet knowing that it is beyond, inaccessible to direct or indirect investigation makes man's access to it at least possible.

Transcendence, Jaspers explains, has its roots in religion as well as in philosophy; these two expressions of man's ascent are, then, closely related to one another, and in fact need one another. Yet they are separate and must maintain their separate ways. Philosophy cannot look for Transcendence in revelation, but must approach Being in the self-disclosures of the Encompassing that are present in man. Thus, the question, "what is Transcendence?" cannot be answered by a knowledge of Transcendence, but rather, through the possibility of man's relating himself to it. *Existenz* is Jaspers' term for this fulfillment of man, and it is achieved by the existential decision.

Man, as we saw before, is always in a situation. This is unavoidable, as are his other ultimate situations—death, struggling, suffering, guilt. When he acknowledges them, his consciousness changes, for he is now face to face with the inescapability of his situation. And in this rebirth of consciousness, he must choose and take up a position within his situation, relating himself to it and acting in it. Jaspers calls this existential choice the "unconditional imperative," breaking the limitation of man's merely empirical existence and constituting his unconditioned self. For the unconditional imperative is an absolutely free act; it precedes every goal or aim, and is therefore not the object of the will, but its source. In following the command of the unconditional, man's decision becomes his substance, the decision *is* him, coming from his very being. Man comes into authentic existence through the imperative because it rises from the Encompassing that he is. In this spontaneity, he arrives at his unconditional foundation—not by degrees, but by a leap—a leap into the Transcendence which is his being.

It is here that communication is so important. Man cannot achieve authenticity in isolation, but only on communication with another who has reached the same level of self-realization. For real communication is a communication of consciousness and in this sense, it produces what it is communicating—consciousness itself. From this, man emerges into being, because consciousness is the path to Existential choice which in turn gives rise to the unconditional.

Yet absolute self-realization is impossible, just as is absolute knowledge. Again, the limits are the "frontiers" of Transcendence, enabling man to recognize where Transcendence is. If he sporadically achieves it, he is still sure to loose it—everything can be betrayed in a moment, yet begun again through the sudden awareness of the unconditional foundations of his being. Every authentic idea of the Encompassing, as well, disappears with each attempt to establish, or isolate, or absolutize it. For there is never any satisfactory, permanent access to Being. This ambiguity and certain frustration is called by Jaspers "foundering" or shipwreck. It is on this note of triumphant failure that Jaspers leaves his philosophy. If man strives and succeeds in his leap to Transcendence, in his passionate attempt to pierce the veils concealing the Transcendent, his efforts will also be shipwrecked at any or every moment because he is finite and as such cannot embrace for long the infinite. Philosophy itself, therefore, becomes important because through it, and its awakening of consciousness, man becomes aware of Being. Through philosophy, the ascent to Transcendence is prepared, and remembered, and in exalted moments, achieved.

Thus in his brief, yet constant experience of Transcendence, man understands that Transcendence *is*; that freedom is; that man, in himself, is inadequate but that Transcendence through the imperative can guide him; and that the world and his life is suspended on an ephemeral thread between God and existence, between hope and uncertainty, between despair and triumph.

A few remarks by way of conclusion may place the work of Karl Jaspers in clearer perspective. It is not our intention in this brief exposition to criticize him in the light of Thomistic philosophy, for to do so in summary fashion would be unfair to both Saint Thomas and to Jaspers as well. We would, rather, simply indicate some weaknesses and point out the lessons that this great philosopher teaches.

It is of interest to note that Jaspers, himself, recognizes a fundamental opposition between Kantian and Thomistic philosophy. There is complex motivation at work in this opposition, he tells us, and what is at stake is "the knowledge of knowledge." Kant teaches that whatever becomes object and knowable by us is not Being Itself but appearance. Saint Thomas' position, on the other hand, holds that our knowledge is capable of grasping Being itself as thought-object. The consequences, Jaspers says, are, first:

> In the Thomistic position I am constantly led to the things, from the sensory object of awareness all the way to the deity; in the Kantian I am led to a point where

the basic operation of my thinking lifts this thinking itself to another level and only thus brings about the presupposition of philosophizing.

He goes on to say:

In the Thomistic position all questioning is dissolved in non-contradictory answers; in the Kantian one arrives at paradoxical assertions concerning the Encompassing. In the Thomistic position the being of finite, sensory being is as good as any other being, even as the being of God; in the Kantian there is a radical difference between appearance and the thing-in-itself. In the Thomistic position particular and total knowledge are differentiated, but both are recognized as knowledge; in the Kantian all knowledge is particular and belongs to the world of appearance; total knowledge is impossible; its place is taken by philosophizing in its soaring to totality as a kind of truth which differs in principle.

Jaspers endeavors to be scrupulously fair in exposing the difference between Kantian and Thomistic noetic, but I feel that he does not do justice to Thomism as a metaphysics of existence and to its related metaphysics of knowledge. He is right, of course, in insisting that Being itself cannot be made into an object, if he means that it cannot be conceptualized. We can, however, know the fact of existence (the existence of any being, not simply human existence) by a complex human cognition which is primarily judicative, forming a judgment of existence.

We would call Jaspers a giant of twentieth century philosophy if the term did not sound so impersonal. From him we may learn much concerning personal and existential communication, the *act* of philosophizing, the deeper recesses of man's being, limit-situations and our finitude, history and the continuity of living tradition. He is sometimes superficially classed as a religious existentialist, together with Gabriel Marcel. He is, in his own eyes, neither theistic nor atheistic, nor religious in any literal or conventional sense. Yet his is a deeply reverent attitude towards the Divine Transcendence, unknowable yet all-encompassing, of which he often speaks in language more Plotinian than Kantian.

He has dedicated his life to research, to thought, and to the problems confronting man in the resolution of his situation. In all of this, Jaspers has affirmed that whatever the approach, method, or result, the fundamental problem is that of discovering whether or not true freedom may be attained by man. He is already recognizable as a unique and irreplaceable figure—a humane and human philosopher. From his writings and his life, from his nobility of mind and magnanimity of spirit, Jaspers is a real witness to the fact that a complete and independent human being is indeed, still possible.

JEAN-PAUL SARTRE

By Joseph Mihalich
LaSalle College

Despite its relatively long history and varied forms of expression, existentialism is largely identified in the popular mind with the life and writings of Jean-Paul Sartre. Sartre enjoyed immense popularity in France immediately after World War II, a popularity not without its shortcomings in that it emphasized the eccentricities of the *avant-garde* rather than the subtleties of Sartre's formal philosophy. Fortunately for all concerned, "left-bank bohemianism" is a transitory and incidental aspect of Sartrian existentialism. A good deal of the popular or mass appeal of Sartrian existentialism is due to two prevalent misconceptions concerning Sartre's approach. One is that his emphasis on complete and unbounded human freedom breeds a kind of fatalistic irresponsibility that licenses or condones any and every human activity, and the other is that his doctrine is a philosophical justification for atheism. It is true that Sartre makes human existence a completely free and wholly unbounded existence, but a concomitant aspect of such existence is a serious and far-reaching responsibility not only to oneself but to all mankind. Sartre asserts that he is an atheist, but he is distressingly frank about the disadvantages of such a proposition. As he points out, without God there is no Absolute Standard or criterion against which we can evaluate our actions and our conduct. We are completely alone "with no excuses behind us or justification before us."

Precisely because of its history and varied forms of expression, existentialism is difficult to describe in a few words. In brief, existentialism is any type of philosophy that centers its analysis on the factor of individual human existence—the fact of the individual's own existence in a concrete and often hostile world. Existentialism's frame of reference in analyzing reality is the individual's own frame of reference—his own fears and hopes and encounters and crises. Existentialism eschews the abstract and the speculative because these aspects transcend the bounds of concrete experience. For the existentialist, *truth* and *being* are not transcendental notions—they are always *my truth* and *my being* as I experience them and give them meaning.

Jean-Paul Sartre was born in Paris in 1905, the son of an officer in the French navy. After a brilliant but erratic scholastic career, Sartre taught philosophy for several years prior to his active participation in the French resistance movement during World War II. Like other existentialists, Sartre expresses himself in novels and plays as well as in formal philosophical texts. The reason for this is that the specific situations in the drama and literature are admirably suited to existentialism's emphasis on the concrete human context as a focal point in the analysis of reality. The dramatic situation is delineated to show the plight of specific individuals faced with specific choices and goals as the means of progress and salvation. Sartre is perhaps best known for his novel NAUSEA, and four short plays—*No Exit, The Flies, Dirty Hands* and *The Respectful Prostitute*. His major philosophical work is BEING AND NOTHINGNESS—"An Essay in Phenomenological Ontology."

If it is possible to sum up Sartre's doctrine in one sentence a statement from NAUSEA would suffice: "Every existing thing is born without reason, prolongs itself out of weakness and dies by chance." This is the kernel of his philosophy in dramatic dress. There is no meaning in existence except the little that the human reality gives it—and the human mode of being is a futile mode in the end. Existence and life and death are all meaningless and "absurd" in that they cannot be explained or in any way justified. Sartre aligns or sets up two regions of being. One is BEING-FOR-ITSELF (*pour-soi*), and the other is BEING-IN-ITSELF (*en-soi*). Being-For-Itself is human reality, and Being-In-Itself is everything else—everything of nature except man. The characteristics of Being-For-Itself or human reality are pure consciousness, absolute freedom. The For-Itself is impersonal, non-substantial, negative rather than positive, and actually *nothing* (no thing)—simply a "hole in being" rather than being itself. The characteristics of Being-In-Itself are immobility and passivity and complete lack of any knowledge or consciousness—just massive being or "dumb packed-togetherness." These two regions are unalterably opposed, and this radical bipolarity is the crux of Sartre's system. The whole existence of the For-Itself is expended in an impossible effort to become something—to become a thing in itself. This is an impossible goal because it would mean a dual contradiction. It is a contradiction to posit the For-Itself as in any way fixed or delineated (as it would be if it were a *thing),* and it is equally contradictory to posit the In-Itself as in any way knowledgeable or conscious. The For-Itself must remain wholly *translucid;* the slightest measure of permanence—even the permanence of an egological structure—is anathema. The For-Itself is thus completely free and unbounded—it is condemned to be free and nothing else. For Sartre, freedom and the human reality are synonymous—to be human is to be free. The For-Itself is pure freedom because it comes from no cause and its sole reason for existing is its constant activity, its constant search for the impossible goal. There is, then, a kind of futility or fatalism in Sartre's human reality, but it is not the popular notion of social or moral or political fatalism. It is a kind of ontological or metaphysical fatalism, stemming from the very nature of the human reality in the hierarchy of things.

The basic thesis in Sartre's thinking is that "existence precedes essence"—we are or exist before we have any specific perfection or nature. We are thrust into being and make ourselves through our actions. Mankind is nothing else except what the individual man makes it to be in making himself through his actions. All this emphasis on human freedom still does not turn it into license. Sartre's philosophy is not developed or intended as an intellectual screen for whim and caprice. We are free—totally and irrevocably free—but not free to do anything we like with no regard for the consequences. On the contrary, such drastic freedom brings with it immense responsibility. Since I make my world in concert with other human realities, the finished product is a concrete manifestation of my wisdom or my folly. The individual human being acts, not in some kind of socio-personal vacuum, but rather within the context of a concrete situation in which he finds himself involved or *engaged*. Our actions in these situations are simply *inventions* in accordance with the demands of the situation. Sartre compares human activity as invention with artistic creativity. He says there are no *a priori* rules of human conduct any more than there are *a priori* rules of art. It is unrealistic to ask with respect to an artist "what painting ought he to make?" The measure of the painting is the degree of correspondence between what the artist intended and the result. The same thing is true of human activity. We have no prior rules or standards to guide our actions and conduct; we *invent* our actions in accordance with the situation as we perceive it. Man the artist and man the ethician have this in common: both are necessarily free and individualistic but neither the work of art nor the human deed is properly arbitrary.

Perhaps the fundamental difficulty in all this is the fact that God does not exist, and so we have no ultimate criterion or Absolute Standard against which we might evalute our actions and our conduct. The only values are human values and the only standards or guides are the standards of each individual within the matrix of his own concrete experience. Every being is alone—tragically alone—with no excuse behind him or justification before him. A significant aspect or concomitant of human activity is what Sartre calls *anguish*. Anguish is the awareness of every human being that we must constantly choose and act, coupled with the realization that nothing and no one can assure us that this is the right choice and the right action. Man makes himself and human nature through his own activity in the concrete situation in which he finds himself, and part of this concrete situation is the awesome realization that upon each choice rests the ultimate happiness and progress of all mankind.

In such a drastic range of freedom for the human reality, there are some apparent restrictions that must be reconciled in some detail. The seeming obstacles to our complete freedom are at least five: 1) our past, 2) our place, 3) our surroundings, 4) our fellow-brethren, 5) our death. On the surface it seems that these items belong to us in such a way—such a concrete way—as to circumscribe us and thus limit our freedom. Sartre's reconciliation of these apparent obstacles hinges on the peculiar notion of the way in which whatever we claim belongs to us or is part of us. We actually *exist* (rather than possess) our attributes and aspects of existence. For example, I do not possess a body or a pain in the head—I *exist* my body and I *exist* the pain in my head. In the same way, I *exist* these apparent obstacles to my freedom in such a way that they are not obstacles at all but rather freely chosen by me.

My *past* has meaning or significance for me (and so delineates me) only if I freely choose to give it significance by freely accepting the *present* which my past has made possible. It is the present rather than the past which is the context of choice and freedom. If I do not freely accept my present then I freely divest myself of the past by changing my present mode or status of existence. If factors in my past have made me at this point in my existence a naval officer, then I freely give my past significance—accept it—by accepting my present status as a naval officer. My past has no unbreakable hold on me because I can reject my past by ceasing to be a naval officer (rejecting my present). Thus I am in control of my past because I am in control of my present. My *place* or location is an obstacle to my freedom only if I make it an obstacle through the choice of an end. If I am a poor worker in Milwaukee and desire to go to Paris, then my place in Milwaukee is an obstacle—but only because of my chosen end or goal. If I choose simply to move from one part of Milwaukee to another, then my place is not an obstacle. The same reasoning applies to my *surroundings*—my tools and equipment. If I freely choose to write a novel, then the laborious hours at the typewriter have a kind of hold on me but only because of my free choice of an end. A boulder on a mountain path is a real obstacle to my progress up the mountain, but the boulder would not have the same status if I had freely chosen to sit at home instead of freely choosing to climb a mountain. It is always the question of my choice of an end that constitutes these aspects of my being as obstacles and hindrances to my freedom.

Regarding my *fellow-brethren* (municipal or religious affiliation and racial derivation) as a possible obstacle to my complete freedom, Sartre says that there are New Yorkers and Parisians and Catholics and Jews and Frenchmen only because certain individuals freely choose to be these things— freely choose to live in New York and Paris and freely accept Catholicism or Judaism. If I do not choose to accept whatever factors of geographical location or race or religion that I find in my concrete situation, then I am free to change them by rejecting these and subscribing to others. Sartre's fundamental premise here is that racial groupings are purely *human conventions* rather than products of nature, and so the fact that I belong to a particular grouping is a matter of my own choosing. My membership in any such grouping is wholly subjective, and thus can be changed if I so desire. The final apparent obstacle to my freedom—my *death*—is the most easily reconciled. My death does not belong to me—it is the outer limit of my consciousness, the last of my possibles. The meaninglessness of death for me is summed up in the phrase that "my death is the one moment of my life which I do not have to live." My death is not for me but for others; it is not my concern, but the concern of others who will notice it and need to deal with it as an aspect of their continuing concrete involvement. Thus not even death is a real obstacle to my complete freedom as a human reality.

The graphic immediacy of the existentialist experience is dramatized in two climactic sequences in Sartre's novel NAUSEA. NAUSEA is the semi-autobiographical story of a French journalist named Roquentin who spends three years in a small French village editing the papers of a dead French politician. In the course of three years, Roquentin experiences gradually more frequent and intensified periods of physical and mental uneasiness—a vague and troublesome feeling which he is at a loss to explain. These mysterious attacks—which he comes to call "the Nausea"—cause him to feel detached and alien in a usually familiar world. The attacks become more and more intense, and finally become so much a part of his existence that they begin to disrupt his work and daily schedule. Then one day he has a kind of revelation in which he comes to understand the Nausea. In an expressive analysis of his state of mind while struck with an attack of the Nausea while sitting in a park, Roquentin comes to realize that the Nausea constitutes his rude awakening to the utter meaninglessness of reality. In his enlightening experience in the park, he perceives that the very presence of the trees and the iron railing and the bench on which he sits is somehow offensive. The objects seem to press in upon him, weighing him down physically with their vaguely vulgar proximity. He notices the root of a tree near his feet and is suddenly revolted by this still object that seethes and writhes with existence. Under his fascinated gaze, this scarred and bark-covered entity comes to symbolize the enigma of all being. From the depths of his Nausea he asks the critical question :"Why should this thing be rather than not be." He finds that he has no answer, and out of his ignorance comes wisdom and freedom from the fear and sickness that plagued him. He realizes that the Nausea was caused by his efforts to see things as others did, to read meaning where there is none. There is no reason why this should be or that should be or anything should be—*it just is.* He sees that the Nausea was the result of his attempts to fight the physical press of existence, inert and powerful existence demanding to be met on its own terms.

The second graphic portrayal of the existentialist experience concerns Roquentin's final visit to his favorite café before leaving Bouville. He has abandoned his editing project as pointless and incongruous in the light of his new analysis of existence. On previous occasions when the Nausea had struck him in the café, he had derived some measure of comfort from listening to a recording of the song *Some of These Days.* He found that the song brought a sense of warmth and happiness, and felt the Nausea vanish as the music "crushed our miserable time against the walls." This was the nub of the question for Roquentin—the utter meaninglessness and futility of our carefully recorded time. On his final visit to the café he asks the waitress to play the recording once more. As he listens for the last time he makes the climactic decision of his life, a decision forced by his solution of the Nausea and the radical insights it has pressed upon him. He perceives that the singer of the song and the author share in the song's perennial potential to convey *meaning,* and that the song serves then as a context in which to escape the utter meaninglessness of routine existence. The existence of the singer and the author is no longer wholly meaningless but is at least partially justified—"not completely of course, but as much as any man can. . . ." Roquentin sees in this a glimmer of hope, a possibility for his own escape from the stark inevitability of being without meaning. He wonders whether he too might justify his existence "just a little" in some creative effort. He determines to write a book—a book that would be "beautiful and hard as steel and would make people ashamed of their existence." Roquentin's decision to write a book (and Sartre's production of NAUSEA) represents an attempt to weave meaning into an existence that would otherwise be as pointless and repugnant as the root in the park. The creative power of the book would perpetuate his memory and mark the fact of his actual existence in this miserable time. His existence would then be justified at least a little and his life could be measured without the repugnance that is part of being without reason. For Sartre the novelist, NAUSEA is metaphysical therapy as well as existentialist literature.

Sartre's philosophy is original (though reflective in some respects of earlier thinkers including Heidegger) and interesting, but philosophically untenable and ultimately inconclusive. One difficulty is the unrealism of the For-Itself or human reality. It conflicts with common experience to portray the human reality as an impersonal and wholly unsubstantial reality, a purposeless "hole in Being." Individual self-existence has a sufficient measure of self-identity and personal integrity to challenge such a view. His arguments against the five obstacles to our freedom leave considerable to be desired. This is especially true of Sartre's conception of arbitrary membership in racial groupings. Granting for purpose of argument that some racial groupings are purely human conventions, groupings on the basis of something like skin coloring would seem to be largely inevitable and impregnable. Another basic difficulty in Sartre's position is the impossibility of any ultimate or transcendent relationship among individuals—any true ethical system. Sartre's human reality exists in an atmosphere of emptiness and enmity, amid overtones of tragedy and futility. The very existence of the other realities is a danger for me, for my absolute freedom flows from my existence as conscious subject rather than dumb object or Being-In-Itself. But other human realities are also conscious subjects and so they tend to regard me as object. When I am reduced to the level of object by someone's gaze or look or knowledge, I lose my most precious attributes—absolute freedom and pure consciousness. So we play a rather serious game with other people in which we attempt to assert our subjectivity while the other attempts to dilute this subjectivity by seeing us a dumb object. The impossibility of a personal ethics in the Sartrian context is dramatized in the often-quoted sequence from Sartre's play *No Exit*. A group of individuals who have passed on from this life are surprised at the nature of their new surroundings: "So this is hell. I'd never have believed it. You remember all we were told about torture chambers, the fire and brimstone, the 'burning marl.' Old wives' tales! There's no need for red-hot pokers. Hell is—other people!"

In a more technical sense, Sartre's existentialism (along with other forms of the same philosophy) suffers from its complete reliance on the *phenomenological method*. The phenomenological method is the description of phenomena—objects and states of consciousness—as they appear to the apprehending subject. Such a method excludes all forms of deduction and *a priori* reasoning as elements in the cognitive process. With deduction and the *a priori* excluded, the only type of analysis possible is the subjective description of phenomena as they manifest themselves to the specific observer in the concrete situation. This necessarily limits the observer to his own personal frame of reference in analyzing himself and all reality. This makes being and knowing a very personal matter of encounter and crisis, but the fact is that there is no logically consistent way in which I can translate my being and my knowing into the universal experience of all mankind. Existentialism's exclusive reliance on the phenomenological method and the exclusion of all speculative and abstract reasoning causes inherent difficulties in the area of metaphysics. In the traditional sense, metaphysics is a science that establishes the ultimate structure of all things. The science of what things *are* (metaphysics) is different from the science of how things are *known* (epistemology). Since phenomenology is primarily the manner of knowing things, it is epistemology rather than metaphysics. To rely exclusively upon phenomenology is to confer upon this method of knowing the nature and purpose of metaphysics. In the traditional view, phenomenologists confuse or identify metaphysics and epistemology. Then *what* we know is identified with *how* we know it.

A serious shortcoming in Sartrian existentialism (and in other forms) is its refusal to give ultimate answers to ultimate questions—e.g., questions of origin and destiny. Sartre puts the general problem of origin and destiny in the context of the absurd (*de trop*) in that they cannot be explained or justified. In his words, things just are—they are or come to be without reason and cease to be or die purely by chance. Philosophy in the best sense of the term is wisdom—the disposition to the knowledge of ultimate first principles and causes and structures of all things. A philosophical system loses something of what it is supposed to be if it arbitrarily stops its investigation with obvious and important phenomena still to be explained. Granting that not every aspect of reality is equally susceptible of explanation and analysis, a consistent pattern of refusal to offer realistic answer to critical questions is not in existentialism's favor. A philosophical system is somehow obligated to suggest something more meaningful than "absurdity" as the ultimate answer to questions of origin and destiny.

From the beginning of philosophy in the pre-Christian era, the goal of every philosophical system is the capacity to solve philosophical problems to the common satisfaction of all men in all times. This testifies to the system's premises with respect to universal human experience and the intelligibility of reality. This is the *philosophia perennis*—"the perennial philosophy." Both traditional philosophy and leading forms of existentialism—Sartre's among them—claim the title of perennial philosophy, though on widely divergent grounds. Traditional philosophy bases its claim on the assertion that reality is a hierarchy of universal essences or natures. The explanation of reality itself is comprised of these constant and unchanging natures and truths—eternal verities conceived in the timeless existence of God as the source of all things. The basis of existentialism's claim to the title is that the most meaningful things to all men in all times is their own personal existence and experiences, and an explanation of reality in terms of these is the perennial philosophy. It is true that existentialism plunges the individual into the vortex of his own experiences and his own multiple cares and worries. But there is more to existence than my own subjectivity, and a philosophical system is not necessarily more realistic because it is more concrete. A true philosophical system should offer the opportunity to fathom universally valid insight into the problems of being and knowing. It is only reasonable to expect that a philosophy oriented to the positive rather than the negative is a more efficacious vehicle for this calculated enlightenment. In order to impart meaning to the world, a philosophical system should first satisfy itself that there is purpose in the world. The authenticity of the *philosophia perennis* lies ultimately in the stability and integrity of the human reality, and the grounding of meaning in the existence of God. Despite all this, Jean-Paul Sartre has undoubtedly assured his place in the history of philosophy as the leading spokesman for the existentialist movement in this century.

GABRIEL MARCEL

By Eugene J. Fitzgerald
La Salle College

The label "Christian existentialism" is an expression coined by others in describing the philosophy of Gabriel Marcel. That he as a person is a devout Catholic and that the general tenor of his writings have much in common with the existentialist concern for the concrete subject, Marcel would scarcely deny. But the ascription "Christian existentialism" could be interpreted to mean a kind of system philosophy, and it is just this connotation that the French thinker wishes avoided in any evaluation of his refreshing quest in the regions of being.

Marcel has said: "All my effort can be described as a straining towards the production of currents by which life is restored to certain areas of the mind which have sunk into torpor and begun to decay." Those responsible for this torpor and decay have attempted to substitute rationalism for life, the absolute idea for the concrete subject, or a gross sensism stripped of its moorings in being and absolutes. In the court of philosophy the villains of the piece are too numerous to mention, but Marcel has no difficulty in recognizing the roles of figures like Descartes, Hegel, and Russell. Because of these deontologizing influences man has been deprived of his wholeness, as well as the charter to know and feel and love as an authentic being. Philosophy, at the least, must re-examine human experience, without apologizing for the avenues it takes and the vistas that it opens up.

Marcel has not always thought this way in his seventy one years. Prior to his conversion to Catholicism at the age of forty he was for the most part a child of the school of classical German idealism. Hegel, Bradley, Royce, and Bergson influenced him in varying degrees. Marcel's theory of participation and involvement, in particular, owe much to Josiah Royce's doctrine of community. That the American Royce fired his mind to a profound extent is evident in the work Marcel brought out on Royce's philosophy of community. Yet he has departed radically from all of the aforementioned thinkers. The earlier part of Marcel's *Metaphysical Journal* begun in the earlier part of this century reveals the idealistic preoccupation with the transcendental, but as his mind wove in and around new labyrinths of experience the reportings in his Journal became less and less tinctured with idealism and increasingly more with the dramatically practical and concrete.

Music and playwriting have been lifelong vocations of Marcel. From Bach he acknowledges his concern for the vitality and pervasiveness of religious experience. And to dramatic writing with its cast of characters caught up in the enactment of life's symphonies, Marcel found himself indebted for the inspiration to depict the immediate, the spontaneous, and the unpredictable in human interaction. Forget these things and Marcel's thoughts become a meaningless and unintelligible kaleidoscope.

If Marcel does not present himself to the philosophical world as a Christian existentialist neither does he care to have his brand of thinking lumped into the general category of what today is called the existentialist movement. However, like all so called existentialists he wishes to establish a humanism which centers on man as a free existent, with all that it implies. Indeed, he believes that the great error of traditional thought has been the reduction of man to the abstract status of an idea. Traditional philosophy has too often looked upon the world as a distinct phenomenon from the self, as though the only legitimate philosophical posture had to be that of theoretical detachment.

Since the central character in philosophy—and philosophizing—must be man regaled in all of his uniqueness, those theories which treat him as a disembodied ego cut off from the soil of his experience (rationalism) or as an intricate piece of sensework alone (empiricism) end up by devaluating the very being which is to be explained. Marcel believes that too often the architecture of philosophy has followed these designs. Idealism, rationalism, and empiricism all have attempted to build monolithic systems. Each has buried man in its debris, with the result that he has been left amorphous and unrecognizable. Modern social and political theories, whether they be democratic or totalitarian, can do the same thing by the cultivation of a mass culture and a technologically oriented mentality. In his more recent works, Marcel complains that one of the great tragedies of twentieth century society is that man can and does become submerged in his function with consequent loss of his freedom and individuality.

Marcel distinguishes between what he calls *mystery* and *problem*. To look at the world in terms of its objective modes without conscious reference to the subjective being of the inquirer or investigator is to consider reality *scientifically*. In the world of problem the investigator is dispassionate, uninvolved personally, and his *job* is to apply special methods and techniques to those things which can be measured, defined, and controlled. The mind passes from one problem to another without attempting to plumb the ontological depth of a situation which may reveal "more than meets the eye."

Mystery by contrast is depth, involvement, and relationship between the subject of the inquiry and his field. Literally, mystery is the prolongation and continuance of the self in that which has no convenient bottom to strike. There

140

is no cry of "Eureka!" here. The quest is endless and resistant to neat conclusions. Such states as grief, love, death, wickedness, fate, and fidelity are illustrative of those situational experiences which properly belong to this broader area of being.

Because being is always infinitely more than we can say about it within any arbitrary frame of reference or methodology, Marcel maintains that metaphysics is the interminable quest of mystery. As a second reflection, the whole content of mystery is neither divulged nor capable of a neat solution. It combines the immediacy of experience with reflection from the subject. Marcel insists that the subject here is an "experiencer" of the whole range of being and never simply an observer of objects. Problem, or first reflection, is the relationship between "me" and "it" where the bond is restricted to subject and object. The reflective posture of intersubjectivity which involves such things as participation, communion, and affectivity characterizes what one might call geography of mystery.

Idealism declares there is no interval between being and the idea of being. "Whatever is real is rational; whatever is rational is real." Accordingly, idealism suffers the fate of all systems which identify being with one of its modes, e. g., *thinking*: it must become atrophied by its false belief that it possesses absolute knowledge. But being is open—it is always encroaching upon itself—and is, in truth, an obscure datum, or that which is yet to be discovered. Seek to grasp it in an idea, no matter how lofty, and one finds himself placidly content with a mirage.

We can see, then, that the key to Marcel's epistemology, and for that matter his whole philosophy, lies in an understanding of what he means by participation. To be is to participate in being. *Esse est co-esse*. The great choice that yawns before man is to become insular or to engage one's self to the rest of being. Since self and that which self participates in cannot be separated, man is organic with the world and it to him.

Marcel indicates that there are different levels of participation:

a) Incarnation—via my body and through sensation
b) Communion—through love, hope, and fidelity
c) Transcendence—through ontological exigence (my need for God)

Incarnation. My existence, or, my existing self, indubitably must include my body. It is through my body that I find myself located in a world of real existence. Now, the body can be considered in two ways: 1) as an object for an observer, or considered as physiological; and 2) as *my* body— which is not an object for any body. The point Marcel is making is that my body and my self are not an instrumental duality. "I *am* my body." The body which is *mine* is not something I *have*. This is the mistake of Plato and Descartes and the psycho-physical parallelists.

Whatever man does, he does as an incarnate being. The body participates in the world and it is through this indispensable channel that the mind is able to experience things as contiguous. Marcel repeats that to be a person one must be in a situation, or in the world participating in being and accessible to being through one's own body (incarnation). Unlike Descartes and the whole tradition of rationalism and idealism, Marcel regards the world as complementary to man. And one's own body plays a two-fold role in this respect: it is a member of the world of things regarded objectively, and it is an integral constituent of oneself.

Platonic idealism and Cartesian rationalism consider the body as a kind of neutral extended substance, different and foreign from the mind which *in fact* is regarded as the real self. But Marcel declares that such a view is a philosophical abomination, creating as it does an impossible dualism which sets up one *essential* component of the entire substance of man against the other essential component. The inordinate intellectualism of thinkers like Descartes, Leibniz, Spinoza and others rule out the *reasonableness* of sensation. Man is always at odds with himself. Even the standard way of interpreting sensation as a kind of translation from physical stimulus to psychic content is erroneous. To admit such would be to establish polarities. Moreover, if it is through the body that I am contiguous with the universe, then it is also through the body and sensation that the human existent stamps his personality on the things around him. Thus, in this theory *things* become more than impersonal objects because of my incarnate relationship with them.

If existence is not an isolated subject severed from the object of its inquiry, neither can it be a predicate searching for a subject. All thought is a mediation within existence. Marcel maintains that existences and the existent must be present to one another from the beginning. A total intelligibility demands no less than this. My situation is the incarnate universe. The thinking self of Descartes is impoverished and suffering from an ontological malnutrition precisely because the being of the thinker is reduced to an essence or a kind of idea.

The individual existent of Descartes and Hegel is universal and anonymous: it never quite makes contact with a world in which it is founded. In a very real sense it is never a singular concrete person breathing the air of subjectivity. But there is still another type of illusory existence. Kierkegaard, Jaspers, and Marcel regard it as an abandonment of the self. The individual is "non-existing." Such a person has an absence of inwardness, a total lack of subjectivity. It is a neutral and amorphous existence of a "thing" among things. Often lucid in his unawareness, this peripheral man never arises above the status of an observer or a spectator. His language is smothered in his obsessions with objects. Heidegger would call him the "ungenuine man." For Ortega y

Gasset, he is regarded as "massmerized." The person so described is comparable to certain cultures which have lost their uniqueness and vitality. Toynbee has called these terrible, frightening paradoxes a life in death.

Marcel indicts our technological society for producing a human anomaly who is lost in his function. Caught up in the complex organization of "occupational" life, the person of man is left fragmented. He does not belong to himself. As representative of the organizational mentality, his mind and freedom and heart are divided and made sterile by the omnivorous economic ethos which dominates the modern age. The monstrous result is that he is a man who has lost his identity.

Marcel's emphasis on the body's role and the importance of sensation has led some critics to accuse him of a sensualism. But this evaluation is hardly fair if one understands the precise way in which Marcel considers sensation. As mentioned earlier, sensation is not merely a message from an alien object to a being who is a receiver. Experimental psychology often regards the phenomenon in such a neutral fashion. Marcel, however, considers sensation as the experience of the mutuality of being. Through his body and the affinity of the senses for other existents man is able to participate in the world by receiving, sharing and giving. Furthermore, sensation allows for man to be *immediately* present to others.

In his philosophy Marcel distinguishes between that which I *am* and that which I *have*. I *am* my body. I *am* my person. Yet, man is constantly tempted to confuse those things which *belong* to him, possessions, with that which could be called his ontological selfhood. Having belongs to the world of objects, and it is entirely possible for the human existent to compromise and neutralize himself by an unbalanced preoccupation with possessions, or objects. Such a concern, Marcel warns, tends to depersonalize the individuality of the subject. To be sure, one *has* a body, but this should not be interpreted to mean that it is an arbitrary possession which can be squandered and misused as an alien object.

"I am my body." To mistreat it or violate it would result in a fatal rupture of the integrity of my selfhood. If the body is a mere possession, then I may consider it as expendable (suicide) or as an indifferent and neutral physiological object which has no essential relationship with my total "being in the world."

Communion. Participation exists not solely through the relationship which one has to his body nor through the vicarious experiencing of others. In a fuller sense, participation is a going out of one's self to the world of being. The awesome power of freedom enables man to be a witness to being, not in an isolated self contained condition, but, rather, as a person who is engaged to the world, responsible to it and for it, and prepared to meet all of its demands within the limits of one's creatureliness.

When one exercises his freedom he commits himself to his choices, and there is the very real possibility that one may lose his hold on existence because of the commitment made and the consequences which ensue from that commitment. It is precisely because of this recognition that Marcel differs so radically from Sartre. Marcel can never forget that man is a creature, and that his very creatureliness imposes both a limitation on his hold of being and generates within himself a fear that he can lose himself.

The human existent of Marcel is prepared for an encounter with the being of others. Contrast this view with that of Sartre's. According to Sartre, man is a stark and lonely splinter of humanity. He stands alone in his uniqueness, but this attribute of singularity must produce a dizziness of desolation. There is no God; therefore, man must make himself. As this naked and solitary existent, man cannot be a creature who is able to acknowledge God and make a vow to be faithful to the demands of one who comes from another. Atheism, then, becomes the only acceptable form of human-

145

ism. But this is not all. Love is out of the question, since it would be contradictory to the anguish and desolation of one who cannot share his being with another.

Nowhere is Marcel more lucid than when he is writing in his rich phenomenological style about communion through love, hope, and fidelity. To love is to place God in the center of our lives, to be able to transcend the immediate and fleeting consciousness of the other based on mere sentimentality. Love is sustained by seeing in the other the richness of the Absolute Thou. It is a pledge to remain faithful even when the immediate and experienced feeling for the other has disappeared.

In love there is truly the existential union of subject and subject. The presence to another subject through my freedom and my love is to make of the other a subjectivity within a subjectivity. I experience him not solely as other, for this would be to restrict the relationship as an analytic one, but rather as an other self. *Alter ego est amicus.* A posture of smug sufficiency is a failure to realize that both myself and those around me owe existence to a common creative fount.

Fidelity bears witness to God and acknowledges His absolute presence. Marriage considered as a sacrament, Marcel tells us, is the highest expression of personal relationship inasmuch as the parties in this noble relationship have called upon God to witness their pledge to remain faithful. But is this merely a pledge? Marcel says no because the continuity of the love can be "guaranteed" by the belief that God will sustain the relationship during catastrophic moments and crises when the shadow of dissolution threatens. More concretely, it is during the numbing situation of a phenomenon like death or separation that we can appreciate the depth of Marcel's observation about the guarantee of the eternity of love.

One's vow to be faithful applies equally to other loves and other relationships. To be rooted in being is to be rooted in God where never ending acknowledgement is *lived out* of

His presence. In this climate and on this soil of being others are not empirical objects which command my attention and bind me in an ephemeral manner. They are related to me because, like myself, they have come from and have their being through the love of God. I can be in a relationship with another and address him in the second person as "Thou." If he is merely an object in a mass then the other never attains more than the status of a neutral "it."

Love is realized through the presence of one to another. It is not simply an intellectual act whereby the other is seen as a cognized object, or better still, as an object among other objects. Presence makes for a reciprocity in relationship. I am available to another, and he to me. Unavailability, Marcel says, is to look upon another with the attitude of alienation. The other is an object, or what could be called when confronted with the suffering of others whom I do not know, for example, a *case* with which I may like to sympathize but which I find not possible because of my indifference. Where one is not at the disposal of others, or unable to experience presence, the individual so detached is both enclosed within himself and unable to free himself from the consequence of his withdrawal.

To be in communion with another involves interpenetration without a loss of being. A person is not a solitary, thinking, enclosed self, but rather one who is *engaged* as an open, communicating being. Ideally, all personal relationship, Marcel believes, should be founded on that genuine cosmic community which the Church calls the Mystical Body. The life of love and communion, therefore, would consist in a constant and newer re-discovery of the truth that we are bound to one another in and through Christ.

Transcendence. Marcel refuses to succumb to the temptation of treating God as an object. "My God" cannot be "caught" in a metaphysical net, as though He were "something out there from me." Instead, we address ourselves to God by translating into language our need for Him. This need for being is our side of transcendence. It is as though Marcel is telling us that God is a presence to be experienced, as a foundation for our creatureliness and contingency. Man is not existence unqualified, but one who participates in being and understands that his total intelligibility requires an absolute acknowledgement of the existence of a Creator.

Marcel resembles St. Anselm and St. Augustine in this respect. If one is to "prove" God let him do it on his knees. "I believe in order that I may know." Outside of such a posture it is possible for God to dissolve into a non-personal Plotinian One so divorced from common being in His transcendence that He is unable to enjoy citizenship in a world where He must also be immanent.

Marcel believes that this is one of the fundamental distinctions between theism and deism. Deism is noble enough, but it does not encompass God as more than a kind of supreme and moral being who presides over the management of the universe. A genuine theism, on the other hand, affirms the possibility of a finite and concrete existent to establish "contact" with a living personal God. God then becomes one who enables me to recognize the grounds of my being and to be able to participate within it. Simply to establish the objective being of God may give me a faint consciousness of Him. However, it is not the same as *knowing* and *believing* that God exists for me.

In a manner reminiscent of St. Augustine, Marcel maintains that to refuse God is a refusal to be. When this happens there is no invocation of God; there is no heed made to the call for plenitude. Just as existence in ontological communion with others is an enrichment of the subject of being, so also is this true when I acknowledge the deep and abiding relationship which exists between myself and God. As the Absolute Thou, God is the guarantee of fullness, plenitude, and transcendence. I have a need to be and only the presence of God can fulfill that exigency.

The question has been asked, and it might be relevant

here, whether there is a radical difference between modern Thomism and the whole existentialist approach of Marcel. While Marcel would not deny the "conclusions" of the classical proofs for the existence of God, he does believe that the attempts at demonstration do not start from an objective uncommitted beginning. Instead, he declares that the "proofs" presuppose an initial acknowledgement of God, as did St. Augustine and St. Anselm. Marcel strongly adheres to the position that God is a presence to be affirmed, not a transcendental object to be grasped with analytical principles which are heirlooms of a past day consciousness. He believes no one can pray to a "pure act" thought of *only* in this abstract manner. There is no doubt that he fears that many modern Thomists are making the mistake of allowing their thinking to be strictured within a Procrustean nomenclature which does little to express the contemporary man's encounter with God and reality.

It is likewise true, however, that Marcel's thought is both enriched and imperiled by his use of the descriptive method. In his investigation of the drama of subjectivity, he finds himself leaning heavily on the language of the theatre and literature which expresses so well man's situational predicament. But therein lies the possibility that his philosophy may have trouble in rising above the novel and dramatic to the heights that real ontological analysis may demand. In answer to all such criticism, Marcel would steadfastly reply that the poetic and metaphysical experience are not as distant and foreign as some traditionalists maintain since true subjectivity incorporates a grasp of both.

The difficulty in articulating a philosophy of subjectivity is that subjectivity *as such* is not a scientific mode of inquiry, as Maritain has said. Being considered as objective, however, may be conveniently handled as scientific data since it can be viewed as universal. Concepts can be handled, treated, and elaborated upon within the framework of a system. Whether Marcel would accuse some modern Thomists of this kind of an evaluation is not here the question that concerns us. What is perhaps very true, however, is that many manuals of Scholastic philosophy have painted being in this fashion. In so doing, these manualists have contracted and thus distorted St. Thomas' full meaning of the act of existing.

St. Thomas was not an existentialist in the present day coinage of that term. But his philosophy invites comparison with all others as the metaphysics of existence. It is a metaphysics which is centered neither on the subjective existent alone nor atrophied to the conceptualized universal as object. The human existent in all the marvelous ways of his subjectivity is not the center of the universe, Aquinas would maintain, but it is God as the supreme existent from whom our being in all of its intelligibility is derived. Not to understand this would dissociate Aquinas from the plan of his *Summa* and the whole depiction of reality he wished to convey. Viewed as a creature, then, man must be seen as coming from Love and returning in his earthly journey toward that source.

If modern Thomism is to remain faithful to a full fledged metaphysics of existence it cannot ignore the vitality of the more positive schools of existentialist thought. Certainly, no one is here advising a "marriage" between the two. But metaphysics runs the risk of distorting the total amplitude of being through inadequacy unless its consciousness is deepened and adapted to the genuine call of subjectivity. In positing the act of being in all its pregnancy the ego is not an anonymous blob. Rather, the ego is an individual who grasps the act of existing as immediately given and suffusing its subjective depths. The being that is real cannot be other than meaningful to the subjectivity of the experiencing self, real and rich and mysterious in itself but at the same time widened to allow for communion with others. In doing so, metaphysics will find a new charter for expression of those principles which are in time and yet are timeless.

SELECTIVE BIBLIOGRAPHY

(Including works by and on the Existentialists)

I. SÖREN KIERKEGAARD

EITHER/OR, A FRAGMENT OF LIFE. Volume one translated by David F. Swenson and Lillian Marvin Swenson; Volume Two translated by Walter Lowrie, 2 vols. Princeton, Princeton University Press, 1944.

REPETITION, AN ESSAY IN EXPERIMENTAL PSYCHOLOGY. Translated by Walter Lowrie, Princeton, Princeton University Press, 1941.

FEAR AND TREMBLING, A DIALECTICAL LYRIC. Translated by Walter Lowrie. Princeton, Princeton University Press, 1941.

STAGES ON LIFE'S WAY. Translated by Walter Lowrie. Princeton, Princeton University Press, 1940.

THE CONCEPT OF DREAD. Translated by Walter Lowrie. Princeton, Princeton University Press, 1944.

EDIFYING DISCOURSES. Translated by David F. Swenson and Lillian Swenson. 4 vols. Minneapolis, Augsburg Publishing House, 1943-46.

PHILOSOPHICAL FRAGMENTS OR A FRAGMENT OF PHILOSOPHY. Translated by David F. Swenson. Princeton, Princeton University Press, 1936.

CONCLUDING UNSCIENTIFIC POSTSCRIPT. Translated by David F. Swenson. Princeton, Princeton University Press, 1941.

PURIFY YOUR HEARTS! Translated by A. S. Aldworth and W. S. Ferrie. London, C. W. Daniel Company, 1937.

WORKS OF LOVE. Translated by David F. Swenson and Lillian M. Swenson, Princeton, Princeton University Press, 1946.

THE SICKNESS UNTO DEATH. Translated by Walter Lowrie. Princeton, Princeton University Press, 1941.

THE JOURNALS. Edited and translated by Alexander Dru. New York, Arford University Press, 1938.

II. *MARTIN HEIDEGGER*

1. *Works by Martin Heidegger*:

DIE LEHRE VOM URTEIL IM PSYCHOLOGISMUS, Diss., Freiburg, 1914.

DIE KATEGORIEN- UND BEDEUTUNGSLEHRE DES DUNS SCOTUS, Habilitationsschrift, Tübingen, 1916.

SEIN UND ZEIT. Erste Hälfte. Halle, 1927. (Appeared first in *Jahrbuch für Philosophie und phänomenologische Forschung,* VIII, 1927, 1-438.)

VOM WESEN DES GRUNDES. *Jb. f. Philos. u. phänom. Forschg.,* Ergänzungsband: Festschrift zum 70. Geburtstag Edmund Husserls (1929), 71-110. Appeared later separately as VOM WESEN DES GRUNDES, 3rd ed. Frankfurt, 1949.

KANT UND DAS PROBLEM DER METAPHYSIK. Bonn, 1929. 2nd ed., Frankfurt, 1951.

WAS IST METAPHYSIK? Bonn, 1929; the 4th ed. appeared 1943, augmented by a *Nachwort;* 5th ed., Frankfurt, 1949.

DIE SELBSTBEHAUPTUNG DER DEUTSCHEN UNIVERSITÄT. Breslau, 1933.

HÖLDERLIN UND DAS WESEN DER DICHTUNG. München, 1937.

PLATONS LEHRE VON DER WAHRHEIT. Geistige Über-
lieferung. Das Zweite Jahrbuch (1942), 96-124.

VOM WESEN DER WAHRHEIT. Frankfurt, 1943; 2nd ed.,
1949.

ERLÄUTERUNGEN ZU HÖLDERLINS DICHTUNGEN.
Frankfurt, 1944; 2nd ed., 1951.

PLATONS LEHRE VON DER WAHRHEIT. Mit einem Brief
über den "Humanismus." Bern, 1947.

HOLZWEGE. Frankfurt, 1950.

EINFÜHRUNG IN DIE METAPHYSIK. Tübingen, 1953.

AUS DER ERFAHRUNG DES DENKENS. Pfullingen, 1954.

VORTRÄGE UND AUFSÄTZE. Pfullingen, 1954.

WAS HEISST DENKEN? Tübingen, 1954.

WAS IST DAS—DIE PHILOSOPHIE? Pfullingen, 1956.

ZUR SEINSFRANGE, Frankfurt, 1956.

IDENTITÄT UND DIFFERENZ. Pfullingen, 1957.

DER SATZ VOM GRUND. Pfullingen, 1957; 2nd ed., 1958.

UNTERWEGS ZUR SPRACHE. Pfullingen, 1959. Contains
essays and lectures.

In English:

EXISTENCE AND BEING. Introd. by Werner Brock. Chicago,
1949.

THE QUESTION OF BEING, tr. by William Kluback. New
York, 1958.

WHAT IS PHILOSOPHY?. tr. by W. Kluback and Jean T.
Wilde. New York, 1958.

AN INTRODUCTION TO METAPHYSICS, tr. by Ralph
Manheim. Yale Univ. Press, 1959.

EXISTENCE AND BEING. Contains an exposition of *Sein und Zeit* by Brock, the essay on Hölderlin, On the Essence of Truth, and What is Metaphysics?.

EXISTENTIALISM FROM DOSTOEVSKY TO SARTRE by Walter Kaufmann, London, 1957. (Contains selection from Heidegger.)

2. *Works on Heidegger*:

Franz Josef Brecht, *Einführung in die Philosophie der Existenz*, Heidelberger Skripten. Heidelberg, 1948.

A. Fischer, *Die Existenzphilosophie Heideggers*. Leipzig, 1935.

Peter Fürstenau, *Heidegger. Das Gefüge seines Denkens*. Frankfurt, 1958.

Marjorie Grene, *Martin Heidegger*. London, 1957.

Hans Jaeger, *"Heidegger's Existential Philosophy and Modern German Literature,"* PMLA. LXBII, 1952, 655-683.

J. Kraft, *Von Husserl zu Heidegger*, Leipzig, 1932.

Thomas Langan, *The Meaning of Heidegger. A Critical Study of an Existentialist Phenomenology*. London, 1959.

Karl Löwith, *Heidegger. Denker in dürftiger Zeit*. Frankfurt, 1953; 2nd ed., Göttingen, 1960.

F. Muth, *Edmund Husserl und Martin Heidegger*. München, 1932.

Johannes Pfeiffer, *Existenzphilosophie. Eine Einführung in Heidegger und Jaspers*. Hamburg., 1949.

Egon Vietta, *Die Seinsfrage bei Martin Heidegger*. Stuttgart, 1950.

A. de Waelhens, *La Philosophie de Martin Heidegger*. Louvain, 1942 and 1946.

Jean Wahl, *Vers la Fin de l'Ontologie. Étude sur l'Introduction dans la Métaphysique par Heidegger*. Paris, 1956.

Beda Allemann, *Hölderlin und Heidegger*, 2nd ed. Zürich and Freiburg, 1954.

Else Buddeberg, *Denken und Dichten des Seins. Heidegger/ Rilke*. Stuttgart, 1956.

III. *KARL JASPERS*

ALLGEMEINE PSYCHOPATHOLOGIE, 1913. 5th ed., 1948, 748 pages. Springer-Verlag, Heidelberg and Berlin.

PSYCHOLOGIE DER WELTANSCHAUUNGEN. 1919. Third edition, 1925. 486 pages. Springer-Verlag, Heidelberg and Berlin.

STRINDBERG UND VAN GOGH. 1922. 131 pages. Third edition, 1949. Joh. Storm-Verlag, Brennen.

MAX WEBER, REDE BEI DER TRAUERFEIER. 1920. 30 pages. Second edition, 1926. Verlag Siebeck, Tübingen.

DIE GEISTIGE SITUATION DER ZEIT. 1931. 191 pages. Seventh edition, 1949. Verlag W. de Gruyter & Co., Berlin. (English translation by Eden and Cedar Paul: Man in the Modern Age, Routledge and Kegan Paul, London, 1951.)

MAX WEBER, POLITIKER, FORSCHER, PHILOSOPH. 1932. Second edition, 1946. 58 pages. Joh. Storm-Verlag, Brennen.

PHILOSOPHIE. 3 vols. 1932. Second edition in one vol. 1948. 913 pages. Springer-Verlag, Heidelberg and Berlin.

VERNUNFT UND EXISTENZ. 1935. New edition 1947. 124 pages. Joh. Storm-Verlag, Brennen.

NIETZSCHE, EINFÜHRUNG IN DAS VERSTÄNDNIS SEINES PHILOSOPHIERENS. 1936. Second edition, 1947. 487 pages. Third edition, 1949. Verlag W. de Gruyter & Co., Berlin.

DESCARTES UND DIE PHILOSOPHIE. 1937. Second edition, 1948. 104 pages. Verlag W. de Gruyter & Co., Berlin.

EXISTENZPHILOSOPHIE. 1938. 86 pages. Verlag W. de Gruyter & Co., Berlin.

NIETZSCHE UND DAS CHRISTENTUM. 1946. 87 pages. Verlag der Bücher-Stube, Fritz Siefert, Hamelin.

DIE IDEE DER UNIVERSITÄT. 1946. 132 pages. Springer-Verlag. Heidelberg and Berlin.

VOM LEBENDIGEN GEIST DER UNIVERSITÄT. 1946. 40 pages. Verlag Lambert Schneider, Heidelberg.

DIE SCHILDFRAGE. 1946. 106 pages. Verlag Lambert Schneider, Heidelberg and at the Artemis-Verlag, Zürich, 95 pages. (English translation by E. B. Ashton: The Question of German Guilt, Dial Press, New York, 1948.)

ANTWORT AN SIGRID UNDSET UND ANDERE AUFSÄTZE. 1947. 31 pages. Südverlag, Constance.

VOM EUROPÄISCHEN GEIST. 1947. 31 pages. R. Piper & Co. Verlag München. (English translation by Ronald Gregor Smith: European Spirit, SCM Press, London, 1948; the Macmillan Co., New York.)

DER PHILOSOPHISCHE GLAUBE. 1947. 136 pages. Second edition 1948. R. Piper & co., Verlag, Munich, and at the Artemis-Verlag, Zurich. 158 pages. (English translation by Ralph Manheim: The Perennial Scope of Philosophy, Philosophical Library, New York, 1949; Routledge and Kegan Paul, London, 1950.)

VON DER WAHRHEIT. 1947. xxiv, 1103 pages. R. Piper & Co., Verlag, Munich.

UNSERE ZUKUNFT UND GOETHE. 1948. 43 pages. Artemis-Verlag, Zürich, and at the Joh. Strom-Verlag, Bremen.

GOETHES MENSCHLICHKEIT. 1949. 33 pages. Helbing & Lichtenhahn, Basel.

VOM URSPRUNG UND ZIEL DER GESCHICHTE. 1949. Second edition 1950. 349 pages. R. Piper & Co. Verlag, Munich. (English translation by Michael Bullock: The

Origin and Goal of History, Routledge and Kegan Paul, London, 1953; Yale University Press, New Haven, 1953.)

PHILOSOPHIE UND WISSENSCHAFT. 1949. 16 pages. Artemis-Verlag, Zürich.

EINFÜHRUNG IN DIE PHILOSOPHIE. 1950. Artemis-Verlag, Zürich. (English translation by Ralph Manheim: Way to Wisdom: An Introduction to Philosophy, Victor Gollancz, London, 1951: Yale University Press, New Haven, 1951.)

VERNUNFT UND WIDERVERNUNFT IN UNSERER ZEIT. 1950. 71 pages. R. Piper & Co. Verlag, Munich. (English translation by Stanley Goodman, Reason and Anti-Reason in Our Time, SCM Press, London, 1952; Yale University Press, New Haven, 1952.)

RECHENSCHAFT UND AUSBLICK; REDEN UND AUF-SÄTZE. 1951. 368 pages. R. Piper & Co. Verlag, Munich.

TRAGEDY IS NOT ENOUGH. 1952. Beacon Press, Boston. (Part III of *Von der Wahrheit*.)

EXISTENTIALISM AND HUMANISM. 1952. Edited by Hanns Fischer, R. F. Moore, New York.

IV. *GABRIEL MARCEL*

1. *Primary Sources*

BEING AND HAVING, trans. by Kaharine Farrer, London, Dacre Press, 1949.

THE DECLINE OF WISDOM, trans. by Manya Harari, London, The Harvill Press, 1954.

HOMO VIATOR, trans. by Emma Craufurd, Chicago, Regnery, 1951.

METAPHYSICAL JOURNAL, trans. by B. Wall, Chicago, Regnery, 1952.

THE MYSTERY OF BEING, 2 vols. Vol. 1, trans. by G. Fraser. Vol. 2, trans. by R. Hague, Chicago, Regnery, 1951.

THE PHILOSOPHY OF EXISTENCE, trans. by Manya Harari, New York, Philosophical Library, 1949.

ROYCE'S METAPHYSICS, trans. by Virginia and Gordon Ringer, Chicago, Regnery, 1956.

THEISM AND PERSONAL RELATIONSHIPS, in Cross Currents, I, Fall, 1950, New York.

2. Secondary Sources

Barrett, W., *"What is Existentialism?"* in Partisan Review, New York, 1947.

Collins, J., *The Existentialists*, A Critical Study, Gateway Edition, Regnery, Chicago, 1952.

Grene, M., *Dreadful Freedom*, A Critique of Existentialism, Chicago, University of Chicago Press, 1948.

Kaufmann, W., *Existentialism from Dostoevsky to Sartre*, New York, Meridian Books, 1956.

Kuhn, H., *Encounter with Nothingness*: An Essay on Existentialism. Chicago, H. Regnery Co., 1949.

Maritain, J.: *Existence and the Existent*, trans. by Lewis Galantiere and Gerald B. Phelan, New York, Image Books, 1956.

Mounier, E., *Existentialist Philosophies*, An Introduction, trans. by E. Blow, London, Rockliff Publ. Corp., 1948.

Troisfontaines, R., *Existentialism and Christian Thought*, trans. by M. Jarrett-Kerr, London, A. & C. Black, 1950.

Wahl, J., *A Short History of Existentialism*, trans. by F. Williams and S. Maron, New York, Philosophical Library, 1949.

V. JEAN-PAUL SARTRE

1. Primary Sources

BEING AND NOTHINGNESS, Gallimard, Paris, 1943.

EXISTENTIALISM, Philosophical Library, New York, 1947.

THE ROADS OF LIBERTY (Ways of Freedom) —A Trilogy:
I. The Age of Reason, Alfred Knopf, New York, 1947.
II. The Reprieve, Alfred Knopf, New York, 1947.
III. Troubled Sleep, Alfred Knopf, New York, 1951.

SITUATIONS I—Gallimard, Paris, 1947.

SITUATIONS II—American Edition—"What is Literature?",
Philosophical Library, New York, 1949.

SITUATIONS III—Gallimard, Paris, 1949.

PSYCHOLOGY OF THE IMAGINATION, Philosophical
Library, New York, 1948.

TRANSCENDENCE OF THE EGO, Noonday Press, New York,
1957.

NAUSEA, NEW DIRECTIONS, New York, 1949.

NO EXIT AND THE FLIES, Alfred Knopf, New York, 1947.
Three Plays by Sartre, Alfred Knopf, New York, 1949:
1. The Respectful Prostitute
2. The Victors
3. Dirty Hands

BAUDELAIRE, New Directions, Norfolk, Conn., 1950.

2. *Secondary Sources*

Allen, E., *Existentialism From Within*, MacMillan, New York,
1953.

Barrett, W. C., *Irrational Man*, Garden City, New York, Double-
day.

Blackham, H. J., *Six Existentialist Thinkers*, Routledge and K.
Paul, London, 1952.

Copleston, F. C., *Existentialism and Modern Man*, Oxford,
Blackfriars, 1948.

Desan, Wilfrid, *The Tragic Finale*, Harvard University Press, 1954.

Harper, Ralph, *Existentialism*, Harvard University Press, 1948.

Laver, J. Quentin, *The Triumph of Subjectivity*, Fordham University Press, 1958.

INDEX